A POPE FOR ALL CHRISTIANS?

A POPE FOR ALL CHRISTIANS?

An Inquiry into the Role of Peter
in the Modern Church

Edited by
Peter J. McCord

PAULIST PRESS
New York/Paramus/Toronto

Library of Congress
Catalog Card Number: 75-32859

ISBN: 0-8091-1918-8

Published by Paulist Press
Editorial Office: 1865 Broadway, N.Y., N.Y. 10023
Business Office: 400 Sette Drive, Paramus, N.J. 07652

Printed and bound in the
United States of America

Contents

62387

This book is dedicated to all the tireless and selfless Christians who have labored amid the trees of their confessions, without losing sight of the forest described by St. Paul:

"There is but one body and one Spirit, just as there is but one hope given all of you by your call. There is one Lord, one faith, one baptism; one God and Father of all, who is over all, and works through all, and is in all" (Ephesians 4:4-6).

*"The pope
—as we all know—
is undoubtedly the gravest obstacle
in the path of ecumenism."*

Pope Paul VI, 1967

Introduction

Robert McAfee Brown

Many Christians today do not find papacy high on their list of immediate ecumenical concerns. Other Christians see it as *the* issue that must be overcome before the ecumenical vision is a reality. The interesting thing is that these two attitudes do not necessarily conflict with one another.

As one who has been straddling both positions, I must confess that I initially approached these essays with some trepidation: how could there be anything more to say on a subject that has already had so much ecumenical ink spilled over it? But the seven essays have overcome my fears. For they exhibit those cardinal qualities of ecumenical discussion, charity and clarity, liberally seasoned with frankness and forthrightness; there is not a sentimental sentence in the book. With a mandate to pull no punches, the authors have followed instructions scrupulously. And yet, the net result is not discouraging but encouraging. While we are a long way from a united church, it is clear that steps like this book will take us farther down the path toward one.

This Introduction is offered neither as an eighth essay, nor as a convenient summary of "the issues" so that indolent readers need read no further than its end. It is simply an overall reflection on the problem of papacy by one who has had the privilege of reading the essays *seriatim* and has been invited to reflect on what he sees and hears.

1

The Contemporary Context of Discussions of Papacy

The context of any discussion of papacy is crucial, for it will set the perspective in which one views the problems and sets his or her own agenda for tackling those problems and determining which, if any, are the really important ones.

The context of the problem of papacy has almost always been intensely ecclesiastical. It has been very much a "churchy" issue, of interest to theologians of several stripes —aggressive Protestants, defensive Catholics, misunderstood Orthodox. It has not been of great interest to outsiders, save when a pope made a statement that seemed to impinge on secular concerns, as the recent furor over *Humanae Vitae* illustrated so tellingly. But if the problem is still ecclesiastical, I suggest that it must at least be viewed within that portion of ecclesiasticism that we call "the church and the world," and that future models of papacy must take seriously not only what papacy means to Christians, but what a certain kind of exercise of papacy might mean to non-Christians as well. We must take seriously that with recent defusings of papal secular power most of the human family simply couldn't care less what Christians decide about primacy or infallibility, and that many Christians will even increasingly wonder what practical difference such discussions can make. We do not live in the "Christendom" era any more, but in the time of the *diaspora*, the dispersion, of the church (as the first essay in this collection reminds us). We live in a time when the burning issues for the human family *and for the church* are going to be centered much more on questions of poverty, hunger, war and racism, than on the subtleties of "real presence," multiple sources of revelation, or fresh nuances on Mary's role in the economy of salvation.

I am a traditional enough theologian to believe that the two sets of issues really overlap and can engage one another in significant ways, but I am also enough of a worldling to realize that the *entré* into the first set of issues is not likely to come solely through the latter. All this is by way of saying that even in our most intricate theological exchanges about the role of papacy, we are obligated to relate the implications of such discussions to the human realities of the great majority of the human family today—non-Christian and non-affluent—who, if they are to be persuaded that theological refinements may contribute to the salvation of the human race, would like to see some tangible evidence of that likelihood. A discussion of papal authority does, as we have learned, impinge on birth control; treatments of Mary may well have implications for women's liberation; papal "style" will have its impact on what we truly believe about poverty; the adoption or rejection of collegiality will say something about how seriously we take the democratic process, and so on. Let no one ignore this broader context of the discussion, or we will find more and more of us talking about topics that matter less and less to most of the rest.

Three Recent Breakthroughs

It may be instructive to look briefly at some important breakthroughs in our understanding of papacy, as a way of particularizing this matter of the context of our discussion. At least three have been of immense contemporary significance.

1. The most pervasive of these was the impact of John XXIII. The world was simply not prepared for the fact that a Roman pope could be so loved—and loved not only by Catholics, but by Protestants, Orthodox and atheists as well, indeed by the whole human family. It is impossible to measure how much this has contributed to the ecumenical thaw after centuries of ecclesiastical cold war. No doctrines were rescinded, no papal powers were foresworn, no new definitions were promulgated that set a new papal style—what happened was simply that the office was engulfed by one who overshadowed many of the preconceptions people had

always thrust upon that office. "If all popes were like that. . ." we began to hear, often wistfully. It is important to realize that Pope John did not resolve or even deal with any of the hard doctrinal issues centering around papacy; he simply persuaded the world that perhaps those issues were once again worth examining.

2. A second breakthrough has been the fact of the Second Vatican Council, coupled with the content of some of its documents. The very fact that the Council was held is important, for it destroyed the pyramidal view of Catholic power and demonstrated—contrary to the anticipations of many after Vatican I—that rule could be shared in the church, rather than lodged unilaterally and exclusively in a single man and office. But substantively as well, the Council moved at least a few theological inches toward a redefinition of the office of papacy. However tentative the move toward "collegiality," especially as expressed in Chapter III of *Lumen Gentium* (the conciliar constitution on the church), a door was opened. One can read the document in question with either a progressive or a conservative emphasis, depending on which points one emphasizes (and the following essays offer interesting examples of the exercise), but there is no gainsaying that a new theme has entered Catholic theology. Papacy is no longer, if it ever was, "one man rule." The pope is head of the episcopal college, but he does not function without the college; the college bears rule in the church, but it does not function without its head. That is, at the very least, not a sheer recapitulation of Vatican I. The results of this new teaching are scarcely auspicious as yet—subsequent episcopal synods have not communicated much assurance that papal power is being shared in collegial fashion. But the door is open. It has not yet opened much further than the Vatican II text, but it would now be exceedingly difficult to close it.

3. A third breakthrough is found in an unlikely event that happened quite contrary to papal design. This was the furor already referred to resulting from the issuing of the papal

encyclical *Humanae Vitae* in 1968. Designed to buttress papal authority by denying that there could be any change in the traditional teaching on birth control, the encyclical had in fact the opposite effect of undermining traditional views of papal authority, since large numbers of the faithful simply refused to adhere to its teaching, hundreds of theologians openly disagreed with it, and many national bishops' conferences made clear, however obliquely, that one could take issue with its content and still be a good Catholic. To some, of course, the response to *Humanae Vitae* has seemed a disaster of epic proportions. Its importance for our discussion, however, is that it has demythologized a certain view of papal authority that has been a vast ecumenical stumbling block, and reinstituted a view that Catholics, in making moral decisions, take into account Scripture, conscience, their own devotional life, and a wide view of tradition, in addition to the strictures of a single document. Many Protestants, Anglicans and Orthodox could live quite comfortably with such a view of papal authority as that now articulated by many Catholics.

We must not minimize the fact that these breakthroughs have been unsettling to the Catholic world. Catholics have seen realities called into question that had been taken for granted for centuries. But a time of unsettling need not be a time of utter dissolution or desolation. There are times when creative rebuilding must be preceded by a certain amount of tearing down. Sometimes, as Jeremiah 45 reminds us, even God himself must tear down what he has built up, in order that new things can emerge and his long-range purposes be fulfilled through them.

Interpretation and Reinterpretation

In such a situation, where do we go? It is clear that things are not going to remain as they were. It is also clear—clearer perhaps than the foregoing comments may have suggested—that the Roman Catholic Church is far from being in its death throes. Formal dogmas are not going to disappear or be jettisoned. Formal dogmas may, however, be subject to further interpretation. In Catholic teaching, the definition of a dogma is not the end of the matter; it is only the beginning of the matter, for there is still the question of interpreting what the dogma *means*. And such interpretation is an ongoing dynamic business; to whatever degree a dogma is close to the heart of a vital truth about the relationship of God and man it can never be exhausted by a few words or even a lot of words. The searching for a fuller, more comprehensive meaning goes on, and in this ongoing process the living tradition of the church continues and grows. (Fr. Dulles' essay, for example, carries on the attempt to look at certain teachings about papacy from a Roman Catholic perspective, while Fr. Meyendorff does the same thing in relation to certain aspects of past church history from an Orthodox perspective.) We are not, in other words, locked in by static interpretations, unavailable for re-examination and reconception. While we can be sure that the reconception will not be so drastic as to destroy the original intent, we can also hope that the reconception will bring to light nuances that may not have been fully apparent in the original intent.

Christian truth, in other words, is dynamic rather than static, and it is important that the ongoing task of interpretation and reinterpretation be carried on for the *whole* of that faith, and not simply limited to a single issue like papacy. Whatever happens in other areas of theological investigation will have a bearing on what we believe about papacy. A continuing look at the overall problem of authority as a problem for *all* Christians, whether Catholic or not, will help us to look at the problem of papal authority in a new way. From a re-examination of the relation of Scripture and tradition, or the authority inherent in ecumenical councils, we can reconceive our contemporary use of the Christian past. Catholics are learning, for example, that there is no clear "papal pattern" in the New Testament, Protestants are learning that the crucial passage in Matthew 16 about the "rock" on which the church will be built almost certainly refers to Peter himself rather than to his faith, while Orthodox are learning that a closer look at the Photian council of 869-870 might provide an important breakthrough between east and west. Such matters can initially be examined on their own merit, and then appropriate conclusions can be drawn for a new understanding of papacy. Each tradition learns that it may have read history through far too parochial eyes, each becomes aware that the very setting of the problem may need to be reconceived, and by that time all are learning that the "locked-in" feeling referred to earlier is of their own construction and can therefore be discarded.

Exercises in Disentanglement

There are other fruitful areas for re-examination. One of these centers on disentangling the juridical and symbolic functions of the papacy. Fr. Meyendorff rightly warns against too great euphoria over symbolic gestures, particularly if the substance of the belief behind the gesture really belies the implications of the gesture; in his telling example, are two churches really "sister churches", as a given symbolic gesture might imply, if the head of one of them appears to be claiming to be the head of both?

It is clear from the non-Roman Catholic essays in this symposium that juridical views of papacy have been particularly difficult for outsiders. Papal power has far too often been entangled with political or even military power for non-Catholics to feel comfortable in its presence. Decisions within the church have appeared to be arrived at unilaterally, and Vatican resistances to collegiality in the decade since Vatican II have been very strong. To cite one other instance, not referred to in the essays that follow, the ambiguous rela-

tionship of the Holy See to the Vatican State is an example
of juridical power that has worried non-Catholics, since the
pope is technically a head of state, a political power himself
in a world of political powers. However anachronistic the
Vatican State may seem (and however unlikely the mobiliza-
tion of the Swiss guard to defend the state against invasion),
there are problems in this political realm that need further
ecumenical exploration. (On this matter, see the essay by
Lukas Vischer, "The Holy See, The Vatican State, and the
Churches' Common Witness: A Neglected Ecumenical Problem," *Journal of Ecumenical Studies*, Vol. XI, No. 4, Fall
1974, pp. 617-636.)

A further matter for more explicitly theological disen-
tanglement is the relationship of primacy and infallibility.
There is a sense in which the primacy of Peter himself is
clear in the New Testament, and even the primacy of the see
of Rome in the early church; what is not so clear is whether
and even how that primacy was extended to Peter's successors,
and whether those successors are the bishops of Rome alone
or the entire college of bishops. The whole issue needs discussion quite apart from the issue of infallibility, since
primacy did not originally involve infallibility. It is quite
conceivable that understandings could be arrived at in the area
of primacy, particularly if, as we shall presently propose,
primacy is fundamentally a primacy of *service*.

But infallibility has subsequently been formally defined by
Roman Catholicism as inhering in the office of the one who
holds the primacy, and that is where the more difficult theological stumbling block is located. The *de facto* likelihood
that infallibility will be invoked by any subsequent occupant
of the see of Peter is so low as to be almost negligible, but
the *de jure* reality remains and must be dealt with. Here particularly the task of asking what a particular dogma *means*
must proceed, for it is far from clear just what the dogma of
infallibility means; there are minimalist interpretations of the

dogma (God will see to it that the church does not proclaim as truth what is in fact error) that many non-Roman Catholics could accept, but there are maximalist interpretations as well, with which even some loyal Roman Catholics have difficulty, and so the dialogue must continue. This is, therefore, an intra-mural Roman Catholic dialogue as well as a dialogue between that church and the other churches of the Christian family. That fact in itself is cause for hope.

Hans Küng has recently advanced views about the meaning of infallibility (in *Structures of the Church, The Church,* and *Infallible? An Inquiry*) that would go a long way toward healing the rupture. As a result, he has been the subject of strong attack from Rome, and yet it is interesting that when judicial proceedings against him were finally concluded, he received little more than a rap on the knuckles. This does not mean that the authorities in Rome approve of Fr. Küng's views; it does mean that they realize that an attempt to silence him (by the exercise of an earlier form of papal juridical power) would be more costly to the church than any conceivable gains to be realized by so doing. So, with at least that (minimalist) negative blessing, the dialogue *can* continue. The present volume helps to advance it.

Servanthood: A Style for Pope and Church

Beyond the strictly theological discussion of papacy, there is a further contribution to resolving the impasse that is more important than might appear at first glance. This has to do with the "style" or symbolism that the papacy—and, by extension, the entire church—conveys. If there is anything that stands out in assessments of the papacy in recent years, it is that the image of pope as *servant* strikes a universally responsive chord among both Catholics and non-Catholics. And if there is anything that stands out in achievements of the papacy in recent centuries it is that the venerable title of *servus servorum Dei* (servant of the servants of God) is not the image that actual popes have projected. Pope John, as we saw earlier, helped to re-establish it, and his so doing generated a new openness to the whole idea of papacy. Significant indications that servanthood was truly to be the new papal style would probably do more to create an atmosphere conducive to theological breakthroughs than any other single thing could.

Unfortunately, the present structures of Catholic life and power militate mightily against the communication of the servant imagery. The pope being carried on the ornate *sedia* on the backs of strong men does not immediately recall an entry into Jerusalem on the unadorned back of a donkey. Nor does the pomp of the papal court call to recollection One who had nowhere to lay his head. It is hard indeed to combine servanthood, i.e., love, and power, but in the one who claims to stand today in Christ's stead, it might well be a top priority. In his play, *The Story of a Humble Christian*, Ignazio Silone recounts the abortive attempt of Pope Celestine V to do this many centuries ago in 1294. He lasted six months. There have been no notable attempts since then, John XXIII excepted. But the symbolic adoption of the servant role would presage a new view of papacy and could elicit new depths of commitment.

This is related to a theological point as well, and one that moves the discussion beyond symbolism. Almost all the essayists in the present volume ask whether or not papacy could be conceived as *primus inter pares*, the pope as "first among equals." Vatican II's doctrine of collegiality sets the stage for a Catholic response to this question in more affirmative tones than has been possible for centuries: the pope needs the college of bishops, the college of bishops needs the pope as its head. The question is: what kind of head? Catholic doctrine could at least move in the direction of *primus inter pares*; whether there is too much else in Catholic history to make the move significant remains to be seen. But such a move would remove many of the Protestant, Catholic and Anglican roadblocks. Papacy as involving primacy of *service* would relate to *primus inter pares* in ways that would be attractive and perhaps even compelling to many who are now resistant.

This brings us back to our original point—the context of the discussion. What is important today, if the pope is to minister truly to a starving and oppressed world, is to conceive of papacy as the embodiment of servanthood. A number of recent papal encyclicals, notably *Mater et Magistra* and *Pacem in Terris* of Pope John, and *Populorum Progressio* of Pope Paul, have focused Catholic thinking on ways in which the church can be servant to the world in matters of hunger, poverty, economic oppression and so on. As these encyclicals help to make clear, neither the church nor the papacy exists for itself; both exist for the sake of the world, embodied in a life of servanthood. There must be a concern to offer both material and spiritual bread to those who are starving. The style of servanthood is the only appropriate style for the Christian family today, and also for the one who is claimed by millions as the head of their particular branch of that family.

This, let it be clear, is not simply a mandate laid upon Roman Catholics or the pope, though the pope can be the most visible embodiment of the new direction of servanthood. It is a mandate placed on the non-Roman Catholic branches of the Christian family as well. It will not be enough for them to mark time while the papacy adapts (the diddling-while-Roman-learns theory). If servanthood is appropriate to the bishop of Rome, it is appropriate to Anglican and Methodist bishops as well, or Orthodox partriarchs, to Presbyterian and Lutheran pastors, to Baptist laity, to Catholic priests, to *all* the faithful. These are directions in which all can—and must—go. My own belief is that such steps would institute a new context for the discussion around which one could build no unscalable walls.

No Fetters on the Holy Spirit

The reunion of a tragically divided church will not come without some breakthrough on the understanding of papacy. We must not presume at this point to know how a breakthrough would come. But we must also not presume at this point to deny that a breakthrough could come. To do the latter would be to seek to bind the Holy Spirit.

We know that it is Christ's will that "all may be one," and that therefore, in the final fulfillment of God's purposes, all *will* be one. So we can continue to work on many fronts —those mentioned in the following essays and many others —confident that somehow, in ways we cannot yet see, all such efforts will be used for good.

Too much has happened ecumenically in the last 15 years to allow us to assume that not much will happen in the next 15—or the next 150. The Spirit still lives.

So the following essays can be offered up confidently, with the prayer: *Veni, Creator Spiritus*—"Come, Spirit-Creator."

Editor's Preface

A few words about the origins of this book may shed some light at the outset on both its content and format.

The idea for the book began in the summer of 1973, born partly out of the editor's sense of frustration with his own church's apparent inflexibility on the subject of authority, as well as a perception that interconfessional differences on church authority seemed to lie at the root of the centuries-long split among Christian denominations. Extensive follow-up reading on ecumenical developments led to the conviction that now, perhaps more than ever before, the principal Christian denominations were more open to interfaith discussion on the greatest ecumenical problem of all: the papacy. The fact that the "Holy Year" of 1975 was fast approaching, focusing attention on Rome and the papacy, seemed to lend the proposed book an added urgency and relevance.

The "symposium" method of presentation resulted from the editor's conviction that discussion of a sensitive interfaith problem could best be treated by employing an "ecumenical" format. The book would thus serve a twofold purpose: first, it would update, for the interested lay reader, the current status of informed ecumenical thinking on church authority; and secondly, it would graphically demonstrate the type of results that can emanate from such an interfaith "gathering" of learned men.

Selecting the "learned men" turned out to be a particularly gratifying task. First to accept, in January 1974, was Avery Dulles, S.J., who had just delivered a paper on "The Papacy as an Ecumenical Problem" and immediately recognized the relevancy of the book's premise. Five months later, the full group had been assembled, each of whom had demonstrated by his prior publications and ministerial activities that he was vitally interested in the cause of Christian unity. To cap off the presentation, Prof. Robert McAfee Brown, author of *The Ecumenical Revolution* (Doubleday, 1969) agreed to write the Introduction.

For his own chapter, each contributor was asked to discuss, first, his denomination's traditional teaching on the subject of church authority, and, secondly, how this teaching impacted on the Roman Catholic concept of church authority as reflected in the teaching on the papacy, i.e., primacy and infallibility. He was then asked to offer some suggestions on what future modifications might be made in Roman Catholic teaching and practice to make it acceptable in some form to his own communion, if at all.

The questions posed to each contributor correspond approximately to those listed in Dr. Burgess' chapter, which appears first in the book. Each author has chosen to address the ecumenical problem of the papacy in his own way, but the questions cited in the Burgess chapter formed the background of each contributor's presentation. And, needless to say, each contributor has presented his personal view as a member of his own denomination, with no official sanction other than his reputation as a theologian, author and minister.

Hopefully, those Christian communities not directly represented by contributing authors will find some threads of continuity from their own confessional point of view and thus feel a sense of participation in this discussion, which was not intended to exclude anyone. Limitations of size, unfortunately, prevented us from having any more contributors.

If, as several of the contributing authors have suggested, a future ecumenical council should ever be called at which *all* Christian churches are invited to participate actively, it would be the editor's hope that this book might perhaps serve both as a partial agenda and as an example of the kind of rational discussion that might result from such a gathering in the spirit of faith-informed charity.

Peter J. McCord
Greenville, South Carolina
Easter, 1975

Lutherans and the Papacy: A Review of Some Basic Issues

Joseph A. Burgess

Has anyone really changed his mind about the papacy? In 1958, during the time of Pius XII, Oscar Cullmann wrote that, from a human point of view, we should have no illusions about the unity of the church as far as Catholics and Protestants are concerned. Neither side ever would or could agree to the concept of church unity held by the other, since that would mean that one or the other would disappear, which neither side was prepared to do. Therefore Cullmann suggested that by means of an offering for the needy on the other side, we might express our Christian solidarity in a minimal way.[1] Today, in view of the widespread hopes that have been raised in discussions about the papacy, we might, on the basis of Cullmann's assumptions, conclude that one side or the other has given up something basic in its view of church unity. But in this problem a change for the better does not necessarily mean giving up something basic.

1. *What does the Lutheran tradition teach regarding the sources or foundations of church authority?*

Along with all other Christians, Lutherans hold that God in Jesus Christ is the final authority. Christ is "the way, the truth, and the life,"[2] and "there is no other name under heaven

17

given among men by which we must be saved."[3] "The first and chief article is this, that Jesus Christ, our God and Lord, 'was put to death for our trespasses and raised again for our justification.' "[4]

The way that Christ is present for us today is through the Gospel. The Gospel is not simply an account of Jesus' words and deeds, nor is it a dogmatic formula; instead, it is the living power of God that effects salvation in the world now.[5] The Gospel not only bears witness to our salvation in Jesus Christ, but it is itself a saving event that breaks into our lives, calling us to faith and discipleship.[6]

This saving event cannot be reduced to a dogmatic formula. Lutherans, however, stress the importance of this event with the expression "justification by grace through faith." All " 'are justified by his grace as a gift, through the redemption which is in Christ Jesus, by his blood.'[7] Inasmuch as this must be believed and cannot be obtained or apprehended by any work, law, or merit, it is clear and certain that such faith alone justifies us."[8] In the words of Luther's explanation to the Small Catechism: "I believe that by my own reason or strength I cannot believe in Jesus Christ, my Lord, or come to him. But the Holy Spirit has called me through the Gospel."[9] "Nothing in this article can be given up or compromised, even if heaven and earth and things temporal should be destroyed."[10] To put it in another, typically Lutheran way: the Law is that which not only curbs the godless, but more importantly shows me my sin and God's judgment; the Law drives me to Christ. Through Christ, without any merit on my part, salvation is mine.

The danger, from the Lutheran point of view, is that justification by grace through faith might be seen as one dogma among others, such as the dogmas about the state, the church, penance, and the like, so that the event of justification is no longer the basis and standard for all proclamation and life in the church.[11] For the event of justification is the event of the Gospel, the power of God in Jesus Christ that not only effects my personal salvation, but everything that is salvation. To be sure, what is meant by the event of justification may be expressed by other words than those in the formula "justification by grace through faith"—for example, by "Jesus is Lord," and "Jesus means freedom." The important thing is to keep the centrality of salvation for the ungodly through Jesus Christ by faith in him alone.

2. *What concrete forms has this authority taken for its function and exercise during Lutheran history?*

Lutherans insist on the primacy of the Gospel. All concrete authority is seen as subject to, and limited by, the "Word of God," which is the Gospel. This does not mean that the church is something invisible and purely subjective; on the contrary, the church actually exists, "made up of true believers and righteous men scattered throughout the world."[12] The criteria for establishing where the church is go back again to the Gospel. The church "is the assembly of all believers among whom the Gospel is preached in its purity and the holy sacraments are administered according to the Gospel."[13] Thus the act of preaching the Gospel[14] and the act of administering the sacraments become the authoritative interpretation of the Gospel. However, the authority does not subsist in the one preaching or administering, but in the fact that Christ has promised to be present in these actions. Because Christ has promised to be present, those doing these things act with his authority.[15]

Lutherans hold to the Bible as the authoritative witness to the Gospel of Jesus Christ, who is the Word of God. The Bible is the only "rule and norm"[16] of all Christian theology. Yet this does not imply a kind of "paper pope," since in the whole Bible "there is nothing other than Christ"[17] and the whole Bible must be understood in terms of Christ.[18]

Lutherans are surprised that others are surprised to discover we also confess the three ecumenical creeds, the Apostles' Creed, the Nicene Creed, and the Athanasian Creed. We pledge allegiance to them as "succinct, Christian, and based upon the Word of God."[19] Practically all Lutherans define themselves as Lutherans by subscribing to Luther's Small Catechism of 1529 and the Augsburg Confession of 1530. Many Lutherans also hold other parts or all of the confessional writings collected in the Book of Concord of 1580.[20] In the Barmen Declaration of 1934 against Nazi ideology,[21] a part of the church made a confessional statement in an emergency situation, and something similar might happen again. However, as Lutherans we hold that every writing, ancient or modern, is subordinate to the rule and norm of Holy Scripture.[22]

Lutherans have also subscribed to the authority of the ecumenical councils, and they have understood such councils to have been held within the first five centuries of the Christian church. At the time of the Reformation Luther and those with him who signed the Augsburg Confession declared that they would only participate in "a general, free, and Christian council."[23] By this they did not mean a council based on theories from the past and called into being by the current pope, but rather a council similar to the German diets and based on Luther's new ecclesiology.[24] Once again, however, Lutherans have contended that councils can err and have erred and again Lutherans have appealed to Holy Scripture as the final authority.[25]

Lutherans know that the Gospel must be proclaimed and that the whole church has the ministry of proclaiming the Gospel. In addition, within the church particular functions exist for the sake of the church and its mission of proclaiming the Gospel. On the one hand, such ministries proclaim the Gospel to the world; on the other hand, by word and sacrament such ministries exhort and reprove within the church. These particular ministries have varied in structure in the past, and they will vary again in structure according to the requirements of the future. But whatever the ministry, it has authority only as it is controlled by the Gospel.[26] For example, the traditional form of authority is the bishop; "according to the Gospel the power of keys or the power of bishops is a power and command of God to preach the Gospel, to forgive and retain sins, and to administer and distribute the sacraments."[27] Thus the bishops have the office of judging doctrine and excluding the ungodly by the power of God's Word, and they are to be obeyed. "However, when bishops teach or ordain anything contrary to the Gospel, churches have a command of God that forbids obedience."[28]

3. *How does Lutheran teaching and its concrete functioning conflict or relate to the Roman Catholic teaching on papal authority, i.e., primacy and infallibility?*

The Papacy and Unity. Pope Paul VI himself has said: "The pope—as we all know—is undoubtedly the gravest obstacle in the path of ecumenism."[29] Lutherans would not put it quite that way. They do not deny that the papacy is a very serious problem and ought to be faced in all of its dimensions. They do not mean to imply that they do not take the unity of the church very seriously or that they would escape from the concrete, visible church into a realm of invisible spirituality. But ever again and always for Lutherans the gravest obstacle in the path of ecumenism is the Gospel.

No one would claim that the papacy is an end in itself. The purpose of the papacy is to bring about the unity of the church. The primacy of the pope therefore is subordinate to unity. But again no one would claim that the unity of the church is an end in itself. It may seem at times in the ecumenical fervor of this century that the unity of the church has become an end in itself, and perhaps in the heat of battle a certain amount of exaggeration is allowable. Nevertheless the unity of the church is not an end in itself. The unity of the church is important only for the sake of the Gospel. Unity is important, to be sure, for it is important that in every way the

Gospel reach into the whole world. Disunity impedes, whereas unity is essential for the mission of bringing the Gospel to the world. But unity, Lutherans would say again and again, is not the Gospel, although unity follows from the Gospel.

Lutherans are of course aware that the church is one, for Christ has but one body. They are aware of what they have in common with most Christians. They have in common the Trinity, Christ, the sacraments of baptism and the Lord's supper, and the ministry of bringing Christ to the world. Unity is something that the church already has. How is it possible for the sake of the Gospel to realize the unity we have, and what is the shape of the unity we seek?

The classic Lutheran answer to these questions is found in the Augsburg Confession: "It is sufficient for the true unity of the Christian church that the Gospel be preached in conformity with a pure understanding of it and that the sacraments be administered in accordance with the divine Word. It is not necessary for the true unity of the Christian church that ceremonies, instituted by men, should be observed uniformly in all places."[30] First of all, it should be noted that it is not a specific dogmatic formulation or set of formulations which is required. To the contrary, it is the actual preaching of the Gospel and actual administering of the sacraments that is "sufficient." Second, such preaching and administering is contrasted with "ceremonies," which here include the dogmatic formulations just mentioned. "It is sufficient" for realizing the true unity of the church that the Gospel actually be preached and the sacraments actually be administered. From the Lutheran point of view, other steps may be taken to shape unity, but they are secondary and certainly not required. No one who knows Lutherans would mistakenly conclude from this position that dogmatic formulations had become irrelevant for the unity of the church. For it is precisely in the continuing process of dogmatic formulation throughout church history that the necessary question of the Gospel is asked: Is what was preached actually the Gospel? and: Is what was administered done according to the Lord's command in such a way that the Gospel is commu-

nicated? Once again, for Lutherans the major ecumenical issue
is the Gospel.[31]

   Because Lutherans have this concern for the unity of the
church, they have been leaders in ecumenical efforts. The
Augsburg Confession of 1530 was one of their efforts.[32] With
respect to the pope himself, the Reformers continued to recognize his legitimate spiritual authority as the bishop of Rome,
and they also conceded his authority by human right over other
churches which voluntarily have attached themselves to him.[33]
In a famous addition to his signature to the Smalcald Articles
of 1537, Melanchthon stated that if the pope "would allow the
Gospel, we, too, may concede to him that superiority over the
bishops which he possesses by human right, making this con-
cession for the sake of peace and general unity."[34] Lutherans
sent delegations to the Council of Trent and hoped to come to
terms with the Roman Catholics even after the peace of Augsburg in 1555. Many Lutheran leaders negotiated with Roman
Catholic representatives for nearly two centuries in an effort to
restore the unity of the church. In the nineteenth century prominent Lutherans continued discussions in order to establish a
united church. In this century the Lutheran World Federation
and Lutheran participation in the World Council of Churches
are indications of Lutheran efforts to restore unity to the
church.[35]

   On the other hand, we dare not pretend that Lutherans did
not oppose the pope. They called him the "antichrist" for
abuses in the use of power and for doctrines and practices
which seemed to them to repudiate the Gospel.[36] Opposition at
times unfortunately led to overreaction, to anti-Romanism for
its own sake. Even today there are Lutherans who, by covert
resistance very similar to the way some whites reject black in-
tegration, want to have nothing to do with ecumenical steps to
restore communion with the Roman Catholic Church. But in
modern times Lutherans have come to discern more and more
the values in the papacy. They appreciate the papacy's historic
assertion of the right of the church to be free from state control, the impact of modern popes on social questions, and the

efforts for world peace made by modern popes from Benedict XV on.[37]

After World War II Lutherans and Roman Catholics in many countries once again began to discuss those questions which separate them. In Germany since 1946 frequent meetings have been held between Lutheran and Roman Catholic theologians; by 1969 the thirtieth encounter in that sequence had taken place.[38] After Vatican II official commissions were established by these two churches. For example, an international Joint Lutheran/Roman Catholic Study Commission met five times between 1967 and 1971 to deal with the topic "The Gospel and the Church," and published its final report in 1972.[39] In the United States twice-yearly meetings began in 1965 between theologians appointed by the United States Roman Catholic Bishops' Committee for Ecumenical and Inter-religious Affairs and by the U.S.A. National Committee of the Lutheran World Federation. These theologians have published reports on the Nicene Creed as Dogma, Baptism, the Eucharist, Ministry, and Papal Primacy,[40] and are currently discussing the problem of Infallibility.

In these more recent discussions Lutherans have reiterated their commitment to church unity. They have pointed to varying factors, such as baptism, the Bible, and liturgies, which have served to unify the whole church. They have also underscored the importance of a specific ministry for the sake of the universal church; it would promote and preserve church unity "by symbolizing unity, and by facilitating communication, mutual assistance or correction, and collaboration in the church's mission."[41] There is no "uniquely legitimate form" for this ministry, for in various ways at various times "councils, individual leaders, specific local churches, credal statements and the papacy have all" ministered to the unity of the church.[42] Thus this unifying function is exercised by whatever "person, officeholder, or local church" ministers to the church as a whole.[43]

The Papacy and the New Testament. This function may appropriately be called a "Petrine function."[44] This does not mean that Peter and those who claim to succeed him have been the only leaders to exercise this function. But Peter undoubtedly enjoyed a preeminence among the apostles during the time of Jesus' ministry and in the post-Easter Church.[45] He was not only the spokesman but also the leader of the apostles; in some passages in the New Testament his words and presence are decisive and authoritative. The frequency with which he is mentioned, the fact that he is very often in the forefront of events, and the emphasis on Peter all indicate that he is not simply another apostle among the Twelve, not simply "first among equals."

For the Gospel of Matthew and the community to which it was written, Peter was the preeminent apostle: in Matthew 14:28-31 Jesus saves Peter as he begins to sink, just as in Matthew 16:18 Jesus builds the church on Peter; in Matthew 16:19 Peter is given the keys and no one else; and in Matthew 10:2 he is called "the first" in the list of apostles. He is in Matthew without question the person in Matthew's church to whom appeal is made as the final authority: in Matthew 15:15 Peter asks Jesus to explain why the disciples are not bound by Jewish food regulations; in Matthew 18:21-22 Peter asks how much the Christian should forgive, a question obviously troubling the Matthean community; in Matthew 17:24-27 the question of the temple tax is brought to Peter who then is instructed by Jesus.

Peter has a place of major importance in the whole plan of Luke-Acts. The story of the miraculous catch of fish and the promise made only to Peter in Luke 5:1-11, plus the promise that Peter's faith will not fail in Luke 22:31-32, both anticipate Peter's prominence after the resurrection, a prominence which is inaugurated by a particular appearance to Peter alone in Luke 24:34. In the first part of Acts Peter leads the early Christian community; in Acts 1:15-26 he proposes and implements replacing Judas among the Twelve; in Acts 2:14-36, 4:8-12, 5:3-16, 10:9-48, and 12:3-17 Peter leads and is prominent, although in Acts 11:1-18 and 8:14 he is possibly accountable to the leaders in Jerusalem, and at times, as in Acts 3:1-11, 4:13, and 8:14, he is paired with John; in Acts 15, in the way Luke has described the Jerusalem council, James and the church may decide, but Peter proposes the solution and on the basis of the fact he had accepted Cornelius into the church. To be sure, in the later chapters of Acts Paul becomes the major figure.

In the Gospel of John and for the Johannine community the "beloved disciple" has a primacy of love. However, although the "beloved disciple" plays a major, coordinate role next to Peter, it cannot be said that the Gospel of John expressly rejects the pastoral authority of Peter.

According to Galatians 1:18 Paul visited Peter in Jerusalem in order to gain information, "to see" Peter; this would indicate that for the Galatians to whom Paul was writing, Peter was some sort of authority in Jerusalem, even though some of the authority may have been the authority of Jerusalem. Various interpretations are held about the disagreement between Peter and Paul in Galatians 2:11-14, but in 1 Corinthians 15:11 Paul affirms the harmony of the apostolic preaching, and in 1 Corinthians 15:5 Peter is first in the list of official witnesses to the resurrection.

Whatever conclusions are reached about the origin and dating of the Petrine literature, in 1 Peter 5:1 Peter is acknowledged as the principal presbyter-shepherd, and in 2 Peter he is the guardian of orthodox faith, for in 2 Peter 1:20-21 he is the one who has the authority to interpret prophecy and in 2 Peter 3:15-16 he even can correct those who misuse Paul's writings.

There is, as is well known, another side to the picture. The Gospels were written primarily as proclamation, as preaching. Peter in the early church is not only pictured as the leader, but also as the typical Christian with all his strengths and weaknesses. Thus in Matthew 14:28-31 Peter is the typical disciple, with exuberant faith, who then fails and sinks, and yet who can count on Jesus to lift him up again; just as he affirms boldly in Matthew 26:35 that he will not deny Jesus, but denies him anyway, and will be lifted up again after the resurrection. In Matthew 16:13-23 Peter is the typical Christian who confesses Jesus, and as long as he confesses Jesus, he is the rock of the church, but as soon as he tries to hinder Jesus with a false understanding of the Messiah, he is no longer the rock of the church but a stone of stumbling, a *scandalon*. In Luke 22:31 it reads: "Simon, Simon, behold, Satan demanded to have you (plural), that he might sift you (plural) like wheat." Here Peter is addressed as the representative of the disciples. He (singular) is then told to strengthen his brothers; but in Luke the verb "strengthen" does not mean "restore to faith," since in Luke the disciples do not lose faith in Jesus, but remain in Jerusalem through the crucifixion. In Luke-Acts "strengthen" means to encourage the Christian community, especially through missionary preaching, as was done by many, such as Paul, Barnabas, Judas called Barsabbas, and Silas. Peter is here the typical, though most prominent, Christian leader. In the Gospel of John, just as the "beloved disciple" is the model for all Christian disciples, so Peter is of competitive importance, a parallel missionary and pastoral model. The question might be raised why precisely Peter often became the model for the "typical Christian" and not another. The answer is that somewhere in early Christendom Peter has become very prominent, so prominent that the Johannine community thought it had to point out that its own "model" was on an equal footing.[46]

Therefore the importance and even preeminence of Peter cannot be denied. At the same time, when all the varying and conflicting factors have been examined, it is evident that the "papacy in its developed form cannot be read back into the New Testament."[47] It is anachronistic to apply terms such as "pope" or "primacy" to the place which Peter held within the New Testament.

Nevertheless, Peter, but also others, did exercise a unifying function in the early church. After the time of the New Testament, however, those who associated themselves with Peter's function continued, while the others disappeared. To what degree is this later development determined by the function which Peter exercised in the New Testament and to what degree is it historical accident? What role does God's providence play in this later development? Conversely, to what degree has this later development influenced how Peter's function has been understood within the New Testament?[48]

The Papacy and History. Lutherans, in spite of their great emphasis on the Bible, do not abandon later church history. We are not innovators. In the Augsburg Confession the Reformers want to make clear that they have introduced nothing "contrary to Holy Scripture or the universal Christian church."[49] And any good index to the Book of Concord will show extensive use by the Reformers of the fathers of the church. Lutherans also are not unaware of the problem of development. They know, for example, that the doctrine of the Trinity is not spelled out in the New Testament. As far as papal claims are concerned, "there is no conclusive documentary evidence from the first century or the early decades of the second for the exercise of, or even the claim to, a primacy of the Roman bishop or to a connection with Peter, although documents from this period accord the church at Rome some kind of preeminence."[50] Even as late as the Council of Nicaea in 325, "a Roman universal primacy of jurisdiction exists neither as a theoretical construction nor as a de facto practice awaiting theoretical interpretation."[51] By the time of Pope Leo I (440-461) the bishops of Rome "have developed a self-image which represents them as the heirs and successors and, in a sense, the continuing embodiments of Peter," but "this view is tolerated in the Christian East when it is in the interest of the East to do so; otherwise it tends to be rejected in practice."[52]

These developments were not isolated from the political and cultural life of the time. Thus the early structure of the church approximated the structures of the Roman empire. In the late medieval period the church was understood as a papal monarchy, following contemporary secular models.[53] Abuses crept in, as the popes became involved in the politics around them, using the often dubious methods of secular diplomacy and even resorting to war. What seemed to early Lutherans to be papal claims of unlimited authority led them to call the pope the "antichrist," a title which both heretics and saints in the medieval period had used to condemn papal abuses.[54] After the Reformation the Roman Catholic Church reacted sharply to nationalism and nineteenth-century liberalism; the papal definitions at Vatican I were shaped by these political and cultural factors. Vatican II, with its insistence on the church as the people of God, on collegiality, and on the pastoral nature of authority, helps to counterbalance the juridical emphasis of Vatican I.[55]

Lutherans, as they look at their own history, do not pretend that it has been immune from political and cultural influences. We too have struggled with nationalism and liberalism, sometimes in a reactionary way. Nor are we unacquainted with ecclesiastical tyranny. Some church leaders, and even pastors in congregations, set themselves up as little "popes," at times because the members themselves want to abdicate their role as the "people of God." On the other hand, as we consider the great changes in the Roman Catholic Church since John XXIII, we no longer label the pope the "antichrist."[56] We are aware of the fact that all churches face a shrinking world, a world in which we as Lutherans dare not let centuries of unconcern about separatism hinder the mission of the universal church.

The Papacy and the Hierarchy of Truths. The *Decree on Ecumenism* of Vatican II states that "in Catholic teaching there exists an order or 'hierarchy' of truths, since they vary in their relationship to the foundation of the Christian faith."[57] Where does the papacy stand in such a hierarchy of truths? Somehow the outsider may suppose that the papacy stands first in the hierarchy of truths, just as it does in the structure of the Roman Catholic Church, but this is not the case. In order to illustrate the actual situation, the sequence may be spelled out:

(a) the primacy of the Gospel. The Gospel is fundamental for salvation; it is the decisive beginning on which all else depends.

(b) the arena of salvation, which is the church. Roman

Catholics recognize that the Eastern Orthodox churches and the Old Catholic Church are part of the arena of salvation, the church with valid episcopacy and valid sacraments, even though allegiance to the pope in Rome is absent. Even Protestant churches according to Vatican II have some sort of ecclesial substance, if not full ecclesial qualifications.[58]

(c) the papacy, a specifically Roman Catholic truth. The papacy exists for the sake of the unity of the whole church, so that the church may more effectively carry out its mission to the world.

Roman Catholics may of course object that distinctions must be made, that the unity of all truth would require that "b" and "c" above must be amalgamated, and that there can be no distinction between Christian truth and the church's truth. Nevertheless, as Rahner has pointed out, the papacy does not belong in "a" but in a "relatively secondary" position in the hierarchy of truths.[59] From the Lutheran point of view what is important about the position of the papacy in the hierarchy of truths is that the Gospel retains primacy; when this is the case, the papacy would not have to be divisive.

A further theological question would be whether the model or paradigm of the "hierarchy of truths" is the only model which could be helpful in discussing the papacy. The problem with the models of "development" and "trajectory" is that both analogies often become more than analogies because of hidden theological agendas. "Development" is used in the exclusive sense of the necessary oak that is hidden in the acorn; the possibility of cancerous growth is not considered. "Trajectory" becomes the path which the projectile necessarily follows, so that from part of the arc the beginning and the ending can be determined; the possibility of another projectile interfering and changing the trajectory is not considered. In the future it might be more helpful to try the familiar model from modern physics of the shift from the world of Newton to the world of Einstein; the change which is presently taking place in the understanding of the papacy might then seem not as alarming to more conservative Roman Catholic minds.[60]

The Papacy and the Model "Iure Divino." The traditional Roman Catholic model has been that the papacy is "divinely instituted" so that it is based on "divine law." What was meant by this in earlier centuries was that Jesus himself instituted the papacy by a formal act and that the New Testament or a tradition from apostolic times clearly attested to that act.[61] Then in 1302 Boniface VIII in the bull *Unam sanctam* concluded that it is necessary for all human beings to be subject to the bishop of Rome for their salvation; this assertion was repeated in 1516 by Leo X at the Fifth Lateran Council, just before the Reformation. In 1537 the Lutheran response was: "The pope is not the head of all Christendom by divine right, or according to God's Word, for this position belongs only to one, namely to Jesus Christ."[62]

Modern Lutherans are also not ready to concede that the pope is "the head of all Christendom by divine right." However, we are able today to make progress toward avoiding the model *iure divino* altogether. Catholic scholarship has helped us to realize that *Unam sanctam* is not a norm for Roman Catholic doctrine because that bull is culturally dated and politically limited; it is not evident from the text itself how it should apply to today, and we are so remote from the historical, social and psychological conditions in which it was written that at best we end up with educated guesses, not doctrinal guidelines.[63] At Malta Lutherans and Catholics agreed that *iure divino* must be seen for the analogy it is; we use the model as if it were possible from a human point of view to distinguish between divine and human law, as if we could escape from the historical process in which we live, but of course we cannot. We only have divine law in particular historical forms. Thus, since we have now become aware of our own historical conditioning, the model is no longer useful.[64] At the same time Lutherans recognize that the Lord works in history through institutional means to bring the Gospel to the world, and while avoiding the model *iure divino*, we too are faced with the question: "What structural elements in the church does the Gospel require for the ministry which serves the unity of the empirical church?"[65]

For their part, Catholics continue to insist that the papacy was instituted "in accordance with God's will."[66] Is it possible for us to understand this insistence in such a way that "in accordance with God's will" does not mean the traditional claim that Jesus himself instituted the papacy by a juridical act? The answer to this question is "yes" if it is understood that "in accordance with God's will" is a functional concept, that it is an "historical and evangelically conditioned instrumental necessity."[67] This means that God wills whatever means are necessary for his church to function in history. The structures that have developed in the church are God's will, first of all because they are in the Bible, but also because God cares for his church. The question is whether such structures are irreversible, that is to say, whether a specific structure such as the papacy is necessarily permanent. Lutherans would reject this claim for the papacy because we see no basis in the Bible for the claim of permanency, although we would agree that God has used the papacy in the past and may do so in the future; however, this implies "contingent necessity," not permanency or irreversibility, for not everything God has used is "irreversibly necessary." The Gospel is of course "irreversibly necessary"; that which functions to unify God's church for the sake of its universal mission is "irreversibly necessary"; but from the Lutheran point of view the historical papacy is "contingently necessary." Some Catholics also adopt this view of the papacy as a "functional" necessity. Others take the position that the papacy is "irreversibly" necessary, and then stress the difficulty of stating exactly what is irreversible in any concrete development, or what degree of jurisdiction is unalterably necessary, because the *divinum* in *ius divinum* inevitably brings in the element of "mystery."[68] It should be obvious to everyone that these different viewpoints overlap and that the model *iure divino* need no longer be a barrier.

Nevertheless, without using the term "divine law," some still appeal to a higher law, the papacy itself. The papacy becomes the source of its own authority. The infallibility of the pope is proclaimed by the pope because he is infallible. The later development becomes the final norm of what it does not find clearly in the earlier development. Authority determines authority authoritatively, in a very tight circle.[69] In this model, the Gospel has lost that primacy which must belong to the Gospel alone.

The Papacy and Infallibility. Lutherans and Catholics at Malta agreed that the church's tradition is always subject to the Word of the Lord, yet at the same time the "Holy Spirit unceasingly leads and keeps the church in the truth." The Gospel is effective when it is proclaimed. Such infallibility is fundamentally a "gift to the entire church as the people of God."[70] The "gates of Hades" shall not prevail against the church.[71] Since the Gospel is effective, the fact that the "gates" will not prevail means more than eschatological indefectibility.[72] The Gospel is already effective here and now.

Difficulties of course arise when Catholics claim that the pope is infallible. But Lutherans are not always aware that Catholics understand the pope to be infallible only within certain limits; at Vatican I the pope's infallibility is defined as being the same infallibility which the church has,[73] not an unlimited infallibility. We Lutherans are confounded at this point by the following sentence, which states that papal definitions are irreformable "by themselves, not by the consent of the church."[74] Catholic commentators assure us, however, that what Vatican I meant is that the pope can act without the formal consent of the church but not that he can act against the consent of the church or in a way which is independent of the Catholic tradition.[75]

Difficulties are further reduced because of the historicity of language and thought forms. Pope John XXIII himself distinguished between the substance of the faith and the form in which the faith is presented.[76] One group or one century may state the faith one way, another group or century another way. What seems to be a barrier proves to be a difference in expression or mode of thought. For example, at the Council of Florence (1439-1442) the Catholic Church recognized that the Eastern churches meant the same thing as the Catholic Church, even though they omitted the "filioque." The same thing is true with regard to certain disagreements from the time of the Reformation; formulas which seemed infallibly to exclude the other side may prove to be differences in language and modes of thought.[77]

Practically all difficulties seem to be removed by proposals from the Catholic side which suggest that dogmas proclaimed during the time when churches were separated, such as the immaculate conception, papal infallibility, and the assumption, should not be made an absolute requirement for the non-Catholic in a future union of the churches, since the non-Catholic has not had the "lived-faith experience" which preceded these dogmas.[78] The non-Catholic, for his part, would be asked if he would "affirm that these doctrines are not contrary to revelation,"[79] and some modern Catholics have interpreted these doctrines in ways which the non-Catholic would find difficult to prove are "unequivocally" contrary to revelation.[80] However, the question remains whether the infallible teaching office would permit some members of a future church union not to be subject to the infallible teaching office. Would not such permission itself be an infallible decision![81] Furthermore, as far as papal infallibility is concerned, no matter how much it is reinterpreted to us by modern Catholic thinkers, finally the Lutheran cannot agree that there is a "divine guarantee against the possibility of the church's teaching office" ever falling into an error which is "unequivocally" contrary to revelation.[82] The Lutheran would hold that the Gospel alone is infallible in this sense.

4. *Are there any conditions under which the Lutheran tradition could accept the Catholic concept of the papacy?*

The only conditions which stand in the way of the Lutheran tradition accepting the papacy are "that papal primacy be so structured and interpreted that it clearly serve the Gospel and the unity of the church of Christ, and that its exercise of power not subvert Christian freedom."[83] This means that Lutherans insist on the primacy of the Gospel. The papacy would be acceptable when it is reinterpreted in such a way that it is subordinate to the Gospel and the unity of the church of Christ. Such conditions seem simple, yet the fact that "primacy" becomes "subordinate" to the Gospel and unity is more than a terminological distinction. The papacy then cannot be in itself the court of last resort because the last resort is the Gospel, the next to the last resort is unity. In a similar vein Lutherans insist that the Gospel means freedom. Since the church in its witness to the Gospel is the arena of this freedom, the church must be an institution of freedom. "Structures which violate this freedom cannot be legitimate in the church of Christ."[84]

But, some Catholics would interject, to act requires power; "the effective exercise of the papal Ministry requires a large measure of power—and power, by its very nature, is capable of being abused." What restrictions could be compatible with the "relative independence" required by "the very nature of the Petrine function to be exercised by the pope"?[85]

Lutherans become uneasy at terminology such as "power," "effective exercise," and "relative independence" with doubtful "restrictions," for we are well aware of the "abuses" that these terms bring in their train. Nor are we reassured by the Catholic disclaimer that any meaningful authority can be abused, and that this is a failure by human beings, not the failure of the church.[86] We are concerned precisely about church structures that prove illegitimate because they violate freedom. That church structures have violated freedom is not disputed. What Lutherans are concerned about is the seeming impossibility of limiting these structures by the prior claims of the Gospel, unity, and Christian freedom. The obvious difficulty with the Catholic suggestion that the pope might voluntarily limit himself through collegial structures[87] is that what one pope might do, the next might undo, perhaps claiming that overriding considerations require it, or whatever. A similar difficulty arises with the suggestion that a pope who might become incapacitated, schismatic, or heretical could be deposed. There exists no regularized form for doing this, but only the fact that in several medieval "emergency" situations which are not binding precedents, popes have been deposed. No matter what theories have been developed about this problem, scholars propose but they do not dispose, even though we would like to suppose they know what would happen. Moreover, theory is far different from practice. Is it possible after Vatican I to depose an absolute ruler who has "executive privileges"?

And yet all this is to take the wrong tack, as though the difficulties would be solved if a satisfactory political formula about power could be developed. As institution the church undoubtedly is involved in power, but not simply raw power, since the church bases its claim on moral power, which by its very nature requires that the person affected by power recognize it to be valid. On this basis the question of power takes on an entirely different dimension. Thus the Catholic ecumenist Lanne, in a discussion of the relationships between the Catholics and the Orthodox churches, suggests that the Catholics need to develop an ecclesiology "based on communion rather than on power and jurisdiction,"[88] and another Catholic, Hermann Häring, points out that an ecumenical Petrine office "must be able, for the sake of the brothers whom it has to serve, to dispense with all privileges, all imperial structures and all power."[89]

There is nothing new in Catholic hopes that the papacy be pastoral rather than juridical, serving rather than served. And the New Testament clearly stresses the difference between worldly power and Christian leadership: "It shall not be so among you; but whoever would be great among you must be your servant, and whoever would be first among you must be slave of all."[90] The difficulty with these Catholic hopes is that there seems to be nothing intrinsic to the nature of the papacy that leads in the direction of such an "angelic pope." With all due respect to the importance of a charismatic leader like John XXIII, the fact that Celestine V (1294) was the last previous pope to be acclaimed in this way indicates that such popes are an accidental rather than a natural result of the papacy. Lutherans would insist that the papacy function in such a way that the primacy of the Gospel, unity and Christian freedom be more than an accidental result or an eschatological hope.

5. *If it were theoretically possible, what structural changes in the Catholic concept of the papacy would have to take place before Lutheranism would consider any kind of formal affiliation? How would such an affiliation take place in practice, i.e., how would the two traditions or churches function together?*

From the Lutheran point of view, church structure is necessary because the church has the mission of bringing the Gospel to a world of space and time, yet the specific form of church structure makes no difference as long as the form does not subvert the Gospel, unity, and Christian freedom. But of course the very practical question still has to be faced: What specific form of church structure would meet these requirements?

In the joint statement made by the Catholic-Lutheran dialogue in the United States, the Roman Catholic Church is asked if it is willing to discuss structures "which would protect the legitimate traditions of the Lutheran communities and respect their spiritual heritage" and if it might "recognize the self-government of Lutheran churches within a communion," in other words, if it would recognize them as "sister-churches."[91] But the very practical question of "how" is still not answered by these proposals.

In that same joint statement Catholics and Lutherans agree on norms for renewal: legitimate diversity, collegiality, subsidiarity.[92] Once again, the question is "how." What happens when, in the eyes of some, legitimate diversity has become divisiveness, collegiality does not lead to agreement, and there is a dispute about what specific powers are subsidiary? How, when faced with those borderline problems which bring primacy and infallibility into play, would these norms work out in practice?

Numerous models have been proposed, such as a geographical center, liturgical or sacramental unity, the various systems of government, and the options suggested by modern corporations. But the fact is that Catholics, while allowing for "changes in the style of papal leadership . . . cannot foresee any set of circumstances that would make it desirable, even if it were possible, to abolish the papal office."[93] Lutherans for their part concede that "institutions which are rooted in history should be seriously considered," for new signs of unity "cannot be invented at will."[94] Then what models are actual possibilities?

First of all, things cannot remain as they are. Furthermore, while Lutherans are concerned to use institutions rooted in history, we cannot foresee any changes in papal style which would serve the Gospel, unity, and Christian freedom and which would not at the same time lead to radical changes in the papal office. Such changes in style could not be merely changes in courtly trappings, for that would not be basic enough. The fact that "whoever would be first among you must be slave of all"[95] describes the New Testament style for serving the Gospel, unity, and Christian freedom, cannot be less than a radical challenge to papal juridical claims.

Second, the uniate model, even under another name and updated, is not acceptable. A uniate church, even if it is permitted many traditions and styles of its own, finally is subject to Roman jurisdiction. Although the term "sister church" might be used, in those borderline cases where primacy and infallibility inevitably are brought in, one sister becomes the "big sister" or the "mother."

Finally, only the future can determine what an adequate model would be. We are of course called upon to theorize about the future, but adequate models are only going to be developed in the future when they are tried and found adequate. For example, Lutherans ask if they might be considered "sister churches," but of course not in the sense of "little sister" as is the case in the uniate model. Is this what Catholics would accept? Ultimately it would have to be tried. Lutherans ask if "the self-government of Lutheran churches within a communion"[96] might be recognized, but of course in the sense that Christian freedom would govern the relationship of Lutheran churches to that larger communion. In the unity of that larger communion would disputed questions be decided by a truly ecumenical council or those whom it might delegate? Again, the proof would be in finding out that the papacy would in fact function in a way which would serve the unity of the larger communion. Lutherans ask if there could be structures "which would protect the legitimate traditions of the Lutheran communities and respect their spiritual heritage."[97] In this question Lutherans are not merely asking about the eucharist in both kinds and a married clergy. The question might be stated in a more concrete fashion: In the unity of that larger communion would the Lutherans be permitted to omit those doctrines which have become official Catholic doctrine after the Reformation, namely the immaculate conception, papal infallibility, and the assumption? It would be understood that Lutherans did not thereby condemn these doctrines, but when these doctrines might become an issue, we would be free to interpret them according to the primacy of the Gospel; the same would be true for any future doctrines which might develop in the Roman Catholic Church unless they were decided by a truly ecumenical council. Once again, in the actual doing of these things it would become evident how serious each side is about the primacy of the Gospel, unity, and Christian freedom.

6. A. 1. *What is the likelihood of such an affiliation taking place in the future? 2. Is it desirable? 3. Is there any indication from current initiatives that the Catholic Church is prepared to make major concessions to bring about such an affiliation?*
B. *What immediate recommendations might be made which would tend to hasten progress in this direction?*

The sad fact is that discussing these questions grows more and more irrelevant. Who cares? Christianity is becoming an ever-increasing minority. Within Christianity itself many are turned off by the ineffectiveness of movements for reform, the hollowness of ecumenical gestures made by many church bodies, and tokenism instead of massive involvement in the problems of the modern world. It is hard to imagine that Christian unity is anything more than the dream of a few who do not face the facts.

Yet who could have predicted John XXIII? Who knows what worldwide tragedy might not drive the churches together? In this post-Constantinian era great changes will overtake the church. Karl Rahner has projected what the church will be like in a future generation. It will be a diaspora, a little flock. There will be no earthly advantage to being a Christian, and Christians will be like brothers and sisters to one another. It will be clear to the Christian of the future that "distinctions of office are necessary but entirely secondary and provisional, transitory things" recognized as "only a burden, a service, a sacred responsibility."[98] What Rahner predicts could happen. Under the pressure of non-Christian and even anti-Christian structures of society, the future church could not afford the luxury of separatism. Cherished distinctions would become irrelevant as future Christians would hold only to the Gospel, unity with each other in Christ, and Christian freedom.

The Russian theologian Solovyof created a more apocalyptic vision of the future union of the churches. In "A Short Narrative about Antichrist" a fictional Russian priest named Pansophia predicts that in the twenty-first century all nations will have been united in one government. The emperor calls a council in Jerusalem to unite the churches; they are to acknowledge him as their Lord. A remnant refuses, denounces the emperor as the Antichrist, and is exiled into the desert. There the venerable John (Orthodox) and Professor Pauli (Evangelical) together submit to Pope Peter II and church unity is restored. The Jews revolt, catastrophe destroys the emperor's forces, and Christ returns.[99] To be sure, some right-wing Protestants have called all church unity anti-Christian because they do not foresee the last half of the vision, and in that case they have a legitimate concern; future church unity could take place for the wrong reasons. But in these "apocalyptic" times Solovyof's vision of the end has a compelling power. A pilgrim church, exiled into the desert or the ghetto, faced with attempts to use the church for non-Christian purposes, would undoubtedly discover and maintain a living unity.

When church unity could finally be achieved may be seen from two points of view. If apocalyptic events intervene, unity may be thrust upon the church. But if things continue as they are, we must think in terms of over a hundred years. Taking a clue from the time that it takes to shift in natural science from one scientific model to another, where such a shift takes from sixty to a hundred years, in the less exact disciplines of theology and church life the process of changing models which we are all involved in will take even longer.[100] Pilot projects will have to be tried, then expanded. It also takes time for intransigents to pass from the scene, and there is a certain inertia which the past thrusts upon the present.

But unity must come, not simply for the sake of mixed marriages and effective mission work. "Our churches should not miss this occasion to respond to the will of Christ for the unity of his disciples. Neither church should continue to tolerate a situation in which members of one communion look upon the other as alien."[101] We are called to be one in the Gospel, in a unity full of the diversity of Christian freedom.

The skeptic may wonder whether anything will be done for unity; vested interests and dogmatism stand in the way. At the moment the tide seems to be running against concrete steps from the Lutheran side, but the Lord may still surprise us. The Roman Catholic Church is retrenching instead of making major concessions. A hopeful sign is the statement recently attributed to Paul VI: "The Roman Catholic Church seems destined to die."[102] That calls to mind the passage in the Gospel according to St. John: "Unless a grain of wheat falls into the earth and dies, it remains alone; but if it dies, it bears much fruit."[103] As Catholics and Lutherans die to themselves, the Gospel, unity, and Christian freedom may come to fruition in our lives.

At the moment what could be done? With all due respect, it should be obvious that changes in trappings lead nowhere. Nevertheless certain steps, little more than symbolic, could make a difference.

1. Create face-saving devices. That is simply asking for tact and diplomacy. The fact that anathemas were not used at Vatican II is already a move in this direction.

2. Luther was excommunicated in 1520. His name is included in the list of heretics read during Maundy Thursday services in Rome. Removing these burdens would simply be to carry on what was begun at Vatican II. For the most part Lutherans already have removed the accusation of "antichrist" against the Roman Catholic Church.[104]

3. Place an age limit on the papacy. In itself this is a small thing, but as a symbolic move it would indicate that permanent limits on the papacy could be imposed.

4. Recognize as valid marriages performed by Lutheran pastors between Lutherans and Roman Catholics.

5. Recognize Lutheran sacraments and orders, and, as a consequence, some kind of altar and pulpit fellowship.

6. Allow Lutherans to take part in papal elections.[105] (It would take courage, for in the United Nations the newer nations have begun to disturb the older nations.) This should include some revision in the process of selecting cardinals, for at present a pope is elected by those whom a pope has selected.

A great yearning for leadership exists in the world. We would ask the Roman Catholics, who stress the papacy's leadership qualities, to take a step forward. We would be easily convinced. Remember how all the world was moved by John XXIII. For our part, we Lutherans "cannot deny that God may show again in the future that the papacy is his gracious gift to his people."[106]

NOTES

1. Oscar Cullmann, *Message to Catholics and Protestants*, trans. J. Burgess (Grand Rapids: Eerdmans, 1959), pp. 22-23, 33.

2. John 14:6.

3. Acts 4:12.

4. Romans 4:25; "The Smalcald Articles," *The Book of Concord*, trans. and ed. Theodore G. Tappert (Philadelphia: Fortress Press, 1959), p. 292 (hereafter cited: Tappert).

5. Romans 1:16.

6. G. Friedrich, "Euaggelion," *Theological Dictionary of the New Testament*, ed. G. Kittel, trans. G. Bromiley (Grand Rapids: Eerdmans, 1964), Vol. 2, pp. 731-733.

7. Romans 3:23-25.

8. Romans 3:26, 28; "The Smalcald Articles," Tappert, p. 292.

9. "The Small Catechism (1529)," Tappert, p. 345.

10. "The Smalcald Articles," Tappert, p. 292.

11. Hermann Diem, *Was Heisst Schriftgemäss?* (Neukirchen: Verlag der Buchhandlung des Erziehungsvereins, 1958), pp. 73-74.

12. "Apology VII and VIII, 20," Tappert, p. 171.

13. "The Augsburg Confession VII," Tappert, p. 32.

14. *Viva vox evangelii.*

15. Luke 10:16.

16. "Epitome, Formula of Concord," Tappert, p. 464.

17. Martin Luther, *Werke.* Kritische Gesamtausgabe (Weimar, 1883ff.), Bd. 11, p. 223 (hereafter cited: WA).

18. Luther, WA 39, I, p. 47; *Deutsche Bibel* 7, 385.

19. "Solid Declaration, Formula of Concord," Tappert, p. 504.

20. See Tappert.

21. "The Barmen Declaration," *Creeds of the Churches*, ed. J. H. Leith (Garden City: Doubleday Anchor Book, 1963), p. 520.

22. "Epitome, Formula of Concord," Tappert, pp. 464-465.

23. "Preface, The Augsburg Confession," Tappert, p. 27.

24. Luther, "De potestate concilii 1536," WA 39, I, pp. 181-197; "Von den Konziliis und Kirchen 1539," WA 50, pp. 509-653. See also Eric W. Gritsch, "Lutheran Teaching Authority: Historical Dimensions and Ecumenical Implications," *Lutheran Quarterly* 25 (1973), p. 385.

25. See also Luther, WA 7, p. 838.

26. *Eucharist and Ministry*, Lutherans and Catholics in Dialogue, Vol. 4 (1970), pp. 9-15; "Report of the Joint Lutheran/Roman Catholic Study Commission on 'The Gospel and the Church,' " *Lutheran World*, 19 (1972), Sections 48-50 and 56, pp. 267 and 268 (cited hereafter: "Malta Report").

27. "The Augsburg Confession," Art. 28, Tappert, p. 81.

28. *Ibid.*, p. 84.

29. Speech to the Secretariat for Promoting Christian Unity, Rome, April 29, 1967, reported in the *National Catholic Reporter*, Vol. 3, no. 28, May 10, 1967, p. 10.

30. "The Augsburg Confession, VII," Tappert, p. 32.

31. Robert W. Jenson, "Dann dies ist genug . . . . Lutheran Conditions for Communion in Holy Things," *Concordia Theological Monthly* 42 (1972), pp. 688-690.

32. "Preface," Tappert, pp. 24-27.

33. "The Smalcald Articles," Part 2, Art. 4, 1, Tappert, p. 298.

34. "The Smalcald Articles," Tappert, pp. 316-317.

35. "Reflections of the Lutheran Participants," *Papal Primacy and the Universal Church*, Lutherans and Catholics in Dialogue, Vol. 5 (Minneapolis: Augsburg, 1974), pp. 27-28.

36. *Ibid.*, p. 25.

37. *Ibid.*, p. 32.

38. Edmund Schlink & Hermann Volk, "Vorwort," *Autorität in der Krise: Veröffentlichung des Okumenischen Arbeitskreises evangelischer und katholischer Theologen*, ed. Gerhard Krems und Reinhard Mumm (Göttingen: Vandenhoeck & Ruprecht, 1970), pp. 7-8; in the same volume, see also: Gerhard Krems und Reinhard Mumm, "Bericht über die Aussprache," p. 151.

39. "Malta Report," pp. 259-260.

40. *Lutherans and Catholics in Dialogue*, Vols. 1-3, ed. Paul C. Empie and T. Austin Murphy (Minneapolis: Augsburg, n.d.); Vol. 4, *Eucharist and Ministry* (published jointly by Representatives of the USA National Committee of the Lutheran World Federation and the Bishops' Committee for Ecumenical and Interreligious Affairs, 1970); Vol. 5, *Papal Primacy and the Universal Church*, ed. Paul C. Empie and T. Austin Murphy (Minneapolis: Augsburg, 1974). This series is cited hereafter as *Dialogue* with the volume number.

41. *Dialogue*, Vol. 5, p. 12; "Malta Report," section 66, p. 270.

42. *Dialogue*, Vol. 5, p. 30.

43. *Ibid.*, p. 11.
44. *Ibid.*
45. *Ibid.*, p. 29.
46. On the whole question of Peter in the New Testament, see "Common Statement," *Dialogue*, Vol. 5, pp. 14-16; "Reflections of the Lutheran Participants," *Dialogue*, Vol. 5, p. 29; as well as the collaborative assessment: *Peter in the New Testament: A Collaborative Assessment by Protestant and Roman Catholic Scholars* (Minneapolis: Augsburg; New York: Paulist, 1973).
47. *Peter in the New Testament*, p. 8.
48. *Ibid.*, pp. 167-168.
49. "Conclusion," Tappert, p. 95.
50. *Dialogue*, Vol. 5, p. 29.
51. James F. McCue, "The Roman Primacy in the Patristic Era: I, The Beginnings Through Nicaea," *Dialogue*, Vol. 5, p. 72.
52. Arthur Carl Piepkorn, "The Roman Primacy in the Patristic Era: II, From Nicaea to Leo the Great," *Dialogue*, Vol. 5, p. 97.
53. *Dialogue*, Vol. 5, pp. 17-18, and the following articles in: *Problems of Authority: An Anglo-French Symposium*, ed. John M. Todd (Baltimore: Helicon; London: Darton, Longman and Todd, 1962): Yves Congar, "The Historical Development of Authority in the Church, Points for Reflection," pp. 119-156; Ian McNeill, "Attitudes to Authority in the Medieval Centuries," pp. 157-167; Patrick McGrath, "Problems of Authority in the Sixteenth and Seventeenth Centuries," pp. 168-176. See also Clemens Bauer, "Bild der Kirche—Abbild der Gesellschaft," *Hochland* 48 (1955/56), pp. 519-527.
54. *Dialogue*, Vol. 5, pp. 25-26.
55. *Ibid.*, pp. 18-19.
56. Wenzel Lohff, "The Papacy and the Reformation: 2, Would the Pope Still Have Been the Antichrist for Luther Today?" *Concilium*, Vol. 4, no. 7, April 1971, pp. 72-73.
57. *Unitatis Redintegratio*, "Restoration of Unity," *The Documents of Vatican II: with Notes and Comments by Catholic, Protestant and Orthodox Authorities*, gen. ed. Walter M. Abbott, trans. ed. Joseph Gallagher (New York: Guild Press, Angelus Book, 1966), section 11, p. 354.
58. Kilian McDonnell, "The Concept of 'Church' in the Documents of Vatican II as Applied to Protestant Denominations," *Dialogue*, Vol. 4, pp. 307-324.
59. Karl Rahner, "Das kirchliche Lehramt in der heutigen Autoritätskrise," *Autorität in der Krise*, p. 104; see also pp. 103-111.
60. T. Howland Sanks, *Authority in the Church, A Study in Changing Paradigms*, American Academy of Religion, Dissertation Series, No. 2 (Missoula, Montana: Scholars Press, 1974), pp. 5-8.
61. "Reflections of the Roman Catholic Participants," *Dialogue*, Vol. 5, p. 34.
62. "The Smalcald Articles," Tappert, p. 298; see also: Arthur Carl Piepkorn, "*Ius Divinum* and *Adiaphoron* in Relation to Structural Problems in the Church: The Position of the Lutheran Symbolical Books," *Dialogue*, Vol. 5, pp. 119-127.
63. George H. Tavard, "The Bull *Unam Sanctam* of Boniface VIII," *Dialogue*, Vol. 5, pp. 117-119.

64. "Malta Report," section 31. See also "Reflections of the Lutheran Participants," *Dialogue*, Vol. 5, p. 31; "Reflections of the Roman Catholic Participants," *Dialogue*, Vol. 5, p. 34.

65. "Reflections of the Lutheran Participants," *Dialogue*, Vol. 5, p. 31.

66. "Common Statement," *Dialogue*, Vol. 5, p. 22; "Reflections of the Roman Catholic Participants," *Dialogue*, Vol. 5, pp. 34-35.

67. George A. Lindbeck, "Papacy and *Ius Divinum:* A Lutheran View," *Dialogue*, Vol. 5, p. 202.

68. *Ibid.*, pp. 193-208.

69. George Tavard, "A Theological Approach to Ministerial Authority," *The Jurist*, 32 (1972), pp. 318 and 328; Karl Rahner, "Das kirchliche Lehramt," p. 109; Charles Davis, "Questions for the Papacy Today," *Concilium*, Vol. 4, no. 7 (April 1971), p. 19.

70. "Malta Report," sections 21-23.

71. Matthew 16:18.

72. George Tavard, "A Theological Approach," p. 326.

73. *Enchiridion Symbolorum: Definitionum et Declarationum de Rebus Fidei et Morum*, ed. Henricus Denzinger & Adolfus Schönmetzer, editio XXXII (New York, Herder, 1963), no. 3074.

74. *Ex sese, non autem ex consensu Ecclesiae.*

75. Roger Aubert, "Die Ekklesiologie beim Vatikankonzil," *Das Konzil und die Konzile* (Stuttgart: Schwabenverlag, 1962), p. 326.

76. "Pope John's Opening Speech to the Council," Oct. 11, 1962. *The Documents of Vatican II*, p. 715.

77. Avery Dulles, *The Survival of Dogma* (Garden City: Doubleday & Co., 1971), pp. 162-169.

78. Joseph W. Baker, "The Petrine Office: Some Ecumenical Projections," *Dialogue*, Vol. 5, p. 220. See also Avery Dulles, "Theologian Asks Lifting of Marian Anathemas," *National Catholic Reporter*, Vol. 11, no. 9, Dec. 20, 1974, p. 2, although Dulles does not include the dogma of papal infallibility.

79. Joseph W. Baker, "The Petrine Office," p. 220.

80. George A. Lindbeck, *The Future of Roman Catholic Theology* (Philadelphia: Fortress Press, n.d.), p. 106, ftnt. 24.

81. See Archbishop Bernardin's reaction to Dulles' proposal: "The final judgment in a matter of this kind must be reserved to the magisterium," quoted in: "Bernardin Cautions on Dulles' Proposal," *National Catholic Reporter*, Vol. 11, no. 9, Dec. 20, 1974, p. 2.

82. George A. Lindbeck, *The Future*, p. 106, ftnt. 24.

83. "Common Statement," *Dialogue*, Vol. 5, p. 21.

84. "Malta Report," section 30.

85. "Reflections of the Roman Catholic Participants," *Dialogue*, Vol. 5, pp. 36-37.

86. Joseph W. Baker, "The Petrine Office," p. 222.

87. "Common Statement: B, Roman Catholic Perspectives," *Dialogue*, Vol. 5, p. 21.

88. Emmanuel Lanne, "The Papacy and the Reformation: 1, To What Extent Is Roman Primacy Unacceptable to the Eastern Churches?" *Concilium*, Vol. 4, no. 7, April 1971, p. 66.

89. Hermann Häring, "Can a Petrine Office Be Meaningful in the Church? 5. An Attempt at a Catholic Answer," *Concilium*, Vol. 4, no. 7, April 1971, p. 141.

90. Mark 10: 43-44.

91. *Dialogue*, Vol. 5, p. 23.

92. *Ibid.*, pp. 19-20.

93. *Ibid.*, p. 37.

94. "Common Statement," *ibid.*, p. 21.

95. Mark 10:44.

96. *Dialogue*, Vol. 5, p. 23.

97. *Ibid.*

98. Karl Rahner, *The Christian of the Future* (New York: Herder and Herder, 1967), pp. 78-80, 100.

99. Vladimir Solovyof, *War and Christianity: From the Russian Point of View, Three Conversations by Vladimir Solovyof,* intro. by Stephen Graham (New York: G. P. Putnam's Sons, 1915), pp. 144-187.

100. T. Howland Sanks, *Authority in the Church*, p. 140.

101. *Dialogue*, Vol. 5, p. 23.

102. James Carroll, "The Church Untriumphant," *National Catholic Reporter*, Vol. 11, no. 8, Dec. 13, 1974, p. 14; Abigail McCarthy, "The Roman Catholic Synod: A Second Look," *New York Times*, Saturday, January 11, 1975, p. 29.

103. John 12:24.

104. To a request by fifty German Catholic laymen and clergy to remove the excommunication, Cardinal Willebrands responded in July 1971 that to do this "is not technically possible." LWF General Secretary Appel objected that although in this case the request was "meaningful" because it came from members of the Catholic Church, it puts Luther's case "on too juridical a level" and that lifting the excommunication "would imply that the differences between our churches are solved" (*LWF information*, Lutheran World Federation News Service, Release No. 41/71, September 15, 1971). However, in view of the fact that on December 7, 1965, Paul VI and Patriarch Athenagoras I mutually voided the mutual anathemas of 1054 (*Herder Correspondence* 3 [1966], p. 38), the technical possibility and symbolic importance of such a removal cannot be denied.

105. Joseph W. Baker, "The Petrine Office," p. 224 for numbers 4-6.

106. "Common Statement: C. Lutheran Perspectives," *Dialogue*, Vol. 5, p. 21.

Papal Authority
in Roman Catholicism

Avery Dulles, S.J.

It is often said that the papacy is the greatest ecumenical problem, at least between Roman Catholics and other Christian groups. This is probably true, but it is no less true in our day that the papacy is a problem for Roman Catholics themselves. By this I do not mean that Catholics today want to do away with the papacy. Most of them, I think, look upon the papacy as a signal blessing for the preservation of the identity and inner cohesion of their own communion. But they have many questions regarding the present mode of operation and the possible future shape of the papacy. These potential metamorphoses of the papacy are intimately connected with its hypothetical role in a reunited Christianity. One cannot speak of an acceptance of the papacy by non-Roman Catholic Christians without some prior consideration of the degree of flexibility compatible with the very notion of papacy.

When we speak of the papacy as an ecumenical problem, therefore, we must not overlook its changing historical forms. To explore these is not to turn aside from ecumenism. Indeed, it is already in some sort an ecumenical exercise. As Georges Florovsky, more than twenty years ago, reminded the Evanston Assembly of the World Council of Churches, there is such a thing as "ecumenism in time."[1] By this he meant, I suspect, that the differences between Christians of diverse eras are not unlike those between diverse confessional bodies. These dif-

48

ferences have to be bridged by the same kind of empathetic and critical mediation that is needed for interconfessional ecumenism. The present chapter will be, for the most part, an essay in this "diachronic" type of ecumenism. Only in the final section will a shift be made to the "synchronic" ecumenical problem.

1. *The Papacy as an Inner-Catholic Problem*

The Roman Catholic doctrine of the papacy, as we know it today, is a product of the nineteenth century. More specifically, it belongs to the pontificate of Pius IX, and it received its most authoritative expression at Vatican Council I (1869-70). That Council, in *Pastor aeternus*, defined under anathema that the papacy is of divine institution, that the pope enjoys a primacy of jurisdiction (and not simply of honor) over all particular churches, pastors, and believers, and that, when he speaks *ex cathedra* as successor of Blessed Peter, he is gifted with infallibility.

The definitions of *Pastor aeternus* depend for their full intelligibility on the historical situation of the Church in Western Europe in the second half of the nineteenth century.[2] It was an era of legitimism and restorationism, when many religious thinkers were in full reaction against the excesses of the Enlightenment and of the French Revolution. Liberalism was seen as the archenemy of the Christian spirit, and faith was extolled as an obedient submission of the mind of man to the revealing word of God. The Church was esteemed as the chief bulwark of divine truth and order against what Newman called "the wild living intellect of man."[3] In some countries, such as Germany and the Austro-Hungarian Empire, efforts had recently been made to give the national hierarchies virtual autonomy from Roman authority. Many Catholics, disturbed by these efforts, and viewing the relative weakness of the Church of England under Queen Victoria, felt the necessity of a strong ecclesiastical government on the international level. They looked to the papacy to give splendor and dignity to the Christian religion and to prevent the Church from being fragmented and manipulated by ambitious political rulers. The idea of a powerful papacy appealed to those who wanted to see the Church prophetically denounce what were thought to be the chief evils of the time—liberalism, nationalism, secularism, relativism, and the like.

It is scarcely surprising, therefore, that the work of Vatican I manifests a rather negative attitude toward the modern world with its glorification of liberty and progress. The Council documents are by our contemporary standards highly authoritarian in tone. Vatican II, meeting almost a century later, reflects a vastly changed situation. By the middle of the twentieth century, the Catholic Church felt itself, in the words of Charles Davis, "culturally estranged from the modern world."[4] For its own vitality and enrichment, as well as for the effectiveness of its mission, the Church saw a real need to participate more fully in the struggles and experiences of the whole human family and to assimilate into its own thinking and practice whatever was healthy in the modern mentality.

If one compares the pronouncements of the two Vatican Councils, one finds clear points of contrast. Vatican I shows a concern for the unchanging identity of the Church and gives little play to historical change and inner pluralism. Vatican II, on the other hand, reflects an acute historical consciousness and a sensitivity to the variety of human cultures. Vatican I speaks in categories that are abstract, scholastic, metaphysical, and juridical. Vatican II prefers to speak in more vivid and concrete language, using historical and empirical categories. Vatican I sees divine truth as coming to the faithful through the mediation of their appointed hierarchical leaders; it suggests a pyramidal model, in which revelation descends from the pope through the bishops to the pastors, who then mediate it by their preaching to the laity. Vatican II accents the value of lay initiatives and the freedom of the Holy Spirit to bestow his charisms as he pleases. Vatican I emphasizes the sufficiency of the Catholic Church as the authorized mediator of the Gospel. Vatican II acknowledges the necessity of openness to values present in the teaching of groups external to the Roman Catholic community. For the authoritarian, defensive stance of Vatican I, Vatican II substitutes a posture of friendliness, self-criticism, and adaptability.

For the contemporary Catholic who fully accepts the attitudes of Vatican II, as here characterized, the doctrine of Vatican I concerning the papacy seems in need of considerable explanation. Many would speak, with Gustave Thils, of the necessity of revision.[5] Revision, however, is a delicate operation since Vatican I laid such heavy emphasis on the irreformability of the divinely given structures and teachings of the Church. In view of the claim of divine institution made for the papacy, it might seem that any significant modification of the doctrine of primacy would fly in the face of the clear teaching of the Council.

A full solution to this difficulty would require a lengthy discussion of the subtleties of hermeneutics. For present purposes, it may suffice to say that dogmatic statements are not immune to hermeneutical treatment. They need to be reinterpreted so as to bridge the gap between the era when they were written—with its own concerns, presuppositions, conceptuality and literary and linguistic conventions—and the interpreter's own era, in which all these variables will have changed. *Mysterium ecclesiae*, a declaration on infallibility issued in 1973 by the Congregation for the Doctrine of the Faith, recognizes the historically conditioned character of dogmatic pronouncements and calls attention to the need of updating them according to the exigencies of the times.[6] The process of reinterpretation is, self-evidently, an unending one. No one interpretation can be imposed as definitive for all future time.

In the following paragraphs an attempt will be made to explore the need and possibility of reinterpreting several of the key tenets of Vatican I: the divine institution of the papal office, the pope's primacy of jurisdiction, and his infallibility.

(a) *Divine Institution*

The question of divine institution became central in the Protestant-Catholic polemical exchanges of the sixteenth century.[7] By and large, both sides agreed that divine institution meant establishment through God's special intervention in history. With reference to the Church this meant, in effect, establishment by the historical Jesus Christ. The assumption was that Jesus had equipped the Church of the first generation with everything essential for its mission to the end of time. Protestants and Catholics, while they were at one in holding that the divine patrimony was permanently sufficient for the Church, disagreed about whether certain ecclesiastical doctrines, offices and rites belonged to this patrimony. They disagreed also regarding the criteria. Protestants generally held that the criterion of divine institution was an explicit dominical injunction contained in Scripture, such as was given in favor of baptism in Matthew 28:19. Catholics replied that there were many things taught by our Lord not written in Scripture but handed down, at least in the early generations, by oral tradition.

With regard to the papacy, Catholics maintained that its divine institution was attested by certain Petrine texts, such as Matthew 16:17-19, Luke 22:32, and John 21:15-17. These texts, as interpreted in the Catholic tradition, referred not simply to the historical Peter, but to his successors to the end of time. The Protestants often denied that these texts established a genuine primacy of Peter among the apostles; quite universally, they denied that these texts could properly be understood as applying to the bishops of Rome.

Today the interconfessional polemics regarding these Petrine texts have considerably abated. Scripture scholars of all traditions are inclined to agree that while many texts, such as those cited above, portray Jesus as conferring upon Peter a certain preeminence among the apostles, nevertheless there is no direct biblical proof for the institution of the papacy as a continuing office in the Church.[8] The idea of an abiding primatial office, or papacy, does not seem to be clearly demanded by Scripture. On the other hand, such a primacy is in no way contrary to Scripture; it is rather favored by those texts which attribute a universal pastoral ministry to Peter.

Can it be maintained that in spite of the lack of any clear biblical attestation, the papacy was specifically instituted by the historical Jesus Christ? The idea that Christ's establishment of this office was known from the beginning and was continuously handed down in oral tradition runs up against the great difficulty that no one seems to have thought of the papacy as a permanent office until about the middle of the third century. Rome did indeed have a certain preeminence among Christian churches, but this status was not ascribed to the fact that Peter had been bishop of Rome or that the pope was Peter's successor in that office. Rather, the emergence of the Roman "primacy" was apparently due to the convergence of a number of factors, e.g., the dignity of Rome as the only apostolic church in the West, the tradition that both Peter and Paul had been martyred there, the long history of Rome as capital of the Empire, and its continuing position as the chief center of commerce and communications. All of these factors helped to confer prestige, wealth, vigor, and influence upon the Roman Church.

Historical investigation shows that the claims made by and on behalf of the bishop of Rome developed very gradually.[9] The crucial period was from the middle of the third century to the middle of the fifth. Even by that time, Rome had a very different relationship to the churches of the West than to those of the East, which had their own apostolic or patriarchal sees to which they looked for direction. As the Eastern churches were subsequently weakened by mutual rivalries, Rome was increasingly called upon to play the role of judge or arbiter. The rise of the Frankish empire in the West and the Muslim pressure on the Eastern churches brought the primacy of Rome to a culmination.

In view of this complicated process of development—all

too briefly summarized in the preceding paragraph—it seems simplistic to speak of the papacy as having been "divinely instituted" in the sense that that term would have had in the sixteenth century. Of course it may plausibly be held, from within the Roman Catholic tradition, that the process of development was divinely intended, or even that it was brought about by some kind of special divine providence; but this is not to claim divine institution for the papacy in the traditional sense. The idea of a providential development, even if admitted, leaves open the question of a possible further development that would leave the papacy behind.

For the modern mind, steeped in historical consciousness, the ancient category of "divine institution" has become problematic. Historically it is most difficult to ascertain just what Jesus did intend for his Church. The New Testament already gives us a picture colored by the theology of the community in a post-resurrection situation. Even if it can be established that Jesus organized his community in some definite way, it does not necessarily follow that he intended to impose that order as an immutable law binding on all future generations. The presumption is rather that he would have intended the Church to be capable of modifying its policy as might be necessary to meet the demands of future generations. The best order for the infant Church might differ radically from the order most suitable for the Church of the nineteenth or twentieth century. Interest today focuses less upon what Jesus "instituted" than upon what form of church order is most viable for our time.

Not surprisingly, therefore, in both the international and American Lutheran-Roman Catholic dialogues, the panels agreed that the concept of "divine institution," so prominent in the sixteenth century debates, is no longer a helpful category.[10] Divine institution implies a rather static or non-evolutionary view of the Church, today rejected by many sophisticated theologians, both Protestant and Catholic.

For a contemporary approach to the problem of the papacy, a more fruitful notion would seem to be that of the "Petrine function" or "Petrine ministry."[11] As already mentioned, many New Testament passages attribute to Peter a particular responsibility for the mission and unity of the Church as a whole. This function, it is argued, is permanently necessary, for if no one is charged with the universal direction of the Church, fragmentation and anarchy cannot be avoided—a consequence to which history bears abundant witness. In theory, the Petrine function could be performed either by a single individual presiding over the whole Church or by some kind of committee, board, synod, or parliament—possibly with a "division of powers" into judicial, legislative, administrative, and the like. Vatican I seems to argue that dissidence will be most effectively precluded if a single individual performs the Petrine function. While this may be true as a general rule, it must also be admitted that ecumenical councils have often had a status in the Church at least equal to that of the popes. In certain crises —e.g., when there is no pope or when there is an unresolved doubt about the identity of the true pope—some other agency than the pope must play the decisive unifying role. Vatican I, which placed supreme authority in the pope, left some uncertainty regarding the relations between the papacy, the universal episcopate, and ecumenical councils (which are not necessarily mere meetings of bishops). Since this uncertainty was not fully cleared up by Vatican II, the question of the supreme directive power in the Church still requires further discussion within the Roman Catholic communion. At present the prevalent assumption seems to be that the pope should have supreme power in the ordinary administration of the Church, but that, in crisis situations, he should convoke ecumenical councils at which all the bishops deliberate and decide with him what course should be pursued. The absence of any constitution or "fundamental law" in the Catholic Church preserves a large measure of vagueness and flexibility regarding the rights and duties of various officers and agencies.

Even the meaning of the term "papacy" is not as clear as might be thought. Catholics generally speak of it as if it were identical with the pope himself, for the pope, at least in theory, has unlimited power over all the Roman Congregations, Secretariats, and the like. In practice, however, these agencies partly escape the pope's control and operate according to their own principles. The inevitability that there be a certain division of labor in the papacy could at some future time call for changes that would make the papacy more like a "constitutional" government, with a legally sanctioned separation of powers. The Catholic Church might experience a constitutional evolution somewhat similar to that of Great Britain, for example, in modern times.

It is often asked whether it is absolutely necessary, according to Catholic doctrine, that the successor of Peter should be the bishop of Rome. Vatican Council I did not wish to condemn the opinion of Bañez and others that the primacy could for good reason be separated at some future time from the Roman See.[12] When the Bishop of Granada requested that the connection between the primacy and the Roman See be defined as being *de iure divino*, he received the reply: "The most reverend Father has spoken learnedly and piously, but not every pious opinion can be inserted into a Dogmatic Constitution."[13] In principle, therefore, it remains open to discussion whether someone other than the bishop of Rome might someday be the primate of the Catholic Church. It would be conceivable, for example, that the bishop of another city might hold the primacy, or that the papacy might rotate among several sees, somewhat as the presidency of the Security Council in the United Nations rotates among representatives of various nations.

From the Roman Catholic point of view, the essential would seem to be that the Petrine function should be institutionalized in some way so that there is in the government of the universal Church an effective sign and instrument of unity. For symbolic efficacy, there are many advantages in having a single person as the bearer of this august office, and in view of the long tradition in favor of Rome as the primatial see, Catholics would be reluctant to see the primacy transferred elsewhere. While understandably attached to the good things in their own tradition, Catholics would be well advised not to assume too easily that the forms of government to which they have become accustomed will necessarily survive the end of time. For the renewal of their own structures, Catholics would do well to attend to the experiences and reflections of other Christian groups who have had to wrestle with the problem of worldwide spiritual authority in their own traditions. Common consultations about such matters can redound to the advantage of all who take part in them.

(b) *Primacy of Jurisdiction*

According to Vatican Council I, the pope, as successor of Peter, has received by divine right a primacy not of honor alone but of true and proper jurisdiction.[14] The jurisdiction of the pope, according to the Council, is universal, ordinary, immediate, truly episcopal, supreme and full.[15]

Quite apart from the question of divine institution, already discussed, these statements are ecumenically difficult, for they run directly counter to the teaching not only of Protestants but also of Anglican and Orthodox Christians, many of whom would be willing to concede that the pope has, at least by human right, a primacy of honor. Increasingly, Roman Catholics themselves have found difficulty in the claim of papal jurisdiction, with all the resounding adjectives attached to it by Vatican I.

Jurisdiction, as the term is currently employed, is a legal term derived from the Roman juridical tradition. It refers directly to relationships within a sovereign state, and is applied to the Church by reason of a certain analogy between the exercise of power in Church and in State. The term became more prevalent as, in the early modern period, the Church took on increasingly the attributes of a political society. But this political model, and consequently the concept of jurisdiction, seems less helpful when applied to the primitive Church or the Church in our own day.

Historically, the attribution of jurisdiction to the bishop of Rome was a gradual development. As Batiffol and others have pointed out, papal influence in the first three centuries had a different character in various zones.[16] In Italy the bishop of Rome exercised strict jurisdiction over all the bishops, whose metropolitan he was. In the remainder of the West (except for certain privileged areas such as Africa), the bishop of Rome was a supermetropolitan, intervening only in *causae majores*. In the East, the churches enjoyed full canonical autonomy under their own metropolitans and supermetropolitans (the future patriarchates). The Eastern churches, however, admitted a certain primacy in the Roman See, to which they accorded what was called a "praecellentia fidei." The churches outside the Roman Empire, such as those of Persia and Abyssinia, had a still more tenuous relationship to Rome.

Only in the Middle Ages, when the Church reacted defensively against the encroachments of the Frankish empire, did something like universal spiritual jurisdiction begin to be claimed for the popes. To St. Thomas in the thirteenth century and Suarez in the sixteenth, it seemed clear that the Church was a strict monarchy in which all bishops depended for their jurisdiction on the positive action of the pope. In the context of opinions such as these, Vatican I maintained that Jesus had conferred on Peter "true and proper jurisdiction" over the entire Church. From the standpoint of the contemporary scholar, it is questionable whether the term "jurisdiction" was a felicitous one, since it seems to juridicize unduly the authority given to Peter. The New Testament, for instance, gives no indication that Peter was empowered by Christ to make laws in the Church, and without this power the modern concept of jurisdiction would not be verified.

Even at Vatican I the concept of jurisdiction was hotly debated. The language of *Pastor aeternus*, in chapter 3, is unquestionably taken from Roman canon law, but the intention, as explained at the Council, was to express a properly theological and scriptural reality. In the course of the debate Bishop Krementz, the future cardinal archbishop of Cologne, emphatically declared:

> The notion of *plenitudo potestatis* is not to be sought from the analogy of worldly powers, or arbitrary and highly subtle explanations of terms, in which everyone finds what he is looking for, but is to be derived from the constitution that Christ the Lord gave to his Church, and the government of this Church cannot be adequately compared to a monarchy, whether absolute or limited, or to an aristocracy or any such thing.[17]

Bishop Federico Zinelli, the official reporter for chapter 3 of *Pastor aeternus*, made the point that the meaning of the term "jurisdiction" in this chapter is qualified by its adjectival modifiers. In particular, he contended, the term "episcopal" should make it clear that the pope's authority is that of a pastor, whose mission it is to feed the flock entrusted to his care. Just as individual bishops are commissioned to feed the particular flocks committed to them, so, Zinelli argued, the pope is commissioned to pasture the whole flock of Christ.[18] Following this line of thought, we may conclude that the universal jurisdiction of the pope as Peter's successor, grounded in Jesus' promises to Peter, is in a very different category from the jurisdiction exercised by a patriarch or metropolitan over some group of churches as a matter of human and ecclesiastical law.

Even with all these qualifications, some Catholics continue to question the appropriateness of the term "jurisdiction" as applied to the kind of authority that the pope should have over the other bishops. As Cornelius Ernst points out, Vatican I posed the question in terms of an opposition between two types of primacy—honor and jurisdiction—so that the term "jurisdiction" was used to exclude a mere primacy of honor.[19] Seen from the perspective of our own day, this dichotomy is unsatisfactory. The authority of Jesus, which according to Matthew 16:17-19 was in some sort transmitted to Peter, cannot be suitably called either honorary or jurisdictional. There is a third kind of primacy, properly theological in nature, to which Ernst gives the name ontological or, in a wide sense, sacramental. In the writings of Leo the Great, he maintains, sacramental themes of primacy predominate over the juridical themes that later become so prominent. In a sacramental view of primacy, the notion of papal power moves away from jurisdiction in the legal sense toward a style of leadership based on charism and moral authority. "What is more, in the providence of God, we have actually had an historical pope in recent years, John XXIII, who has given us a personal expression of that original unity, perhaps because personal sanctity alone is the only valid means of discovering and disclosing it."[20]

Some ecumenical theologians, since Vatican II, point out that the notion of a "primacy of honor" is capable of being defended, even from within the Roman Catholic tradition. The pope, like a patriarch, is not a superbishop; he is a bishop among bishops. He exercises a primacy not over bishops but rather among bishops and is, in that sense, a first among equals. He may be said to have a primacy of honor, provided it be recognized, as Père Duprey reminds us, that there is no honor in the Church except in view of a service.[21] The special service of the universal primate, viewed in the ecclesiological perspectives of Vatican II, is "to preside over the assembly of charity"[22] and to foster collegial relationships among the regional bishops and particular churches. This idea, suitably explained, might remove some of the difficulties continually raised, especially in the East, against the concept of a primacy of jurisdiction. It would permit the concept of papal primacy to be interpreted less legalistically and more in accord with a collegial or conciliar vision of the Church. For one member of a college to exercise jurisdiction, in a political sense, over all the others would seem to destroy the fundamental equality that is the very basis of collegial relationships.

(c) *Infallibility*

From the standpoint of our times, the most offensive of all the papal definitions at Vatican I is the dogma of papal infallibility. The idea that the truth of revelation could be pinned down in a dogmatic formula, binding on all future generations, seems to many of our contemporaries quite intolerable. The scandal is increased by the Council's affirmation that papal statements enjoy such infallibility "by themselves and not by the consent of the Church."[23]

Once again, we are faced with the effects of a cultural shift. At the time of Vatican I, infallibility as such was not a crucial problem. The Council saw no necessity to explore the notions of infallibility and irreformability, for it was taken for granted by all parties in the Church that the supreme magisterium, as the decisive organ of revelation, must be able to speak infallibly, in such a way that its pronouncements would be "irreformable." The main question under debate was the locus of the supreme, infallible teaching power. Did the pope have it by himself, or did he have it only—as the Gallicans had contended[24]—when the national hierarchies or the universal episcopate concurred? In answer to this question the Council affirmed that the pope himself, under certain conditions, enjoys "that infallibility with which the divine Redeemer willed his Church to be equipped in defining the teaching of faith and morals."[25] This statement leaves open the tremendous question what kind and measure of infallibility Christ did choose to confer upon his Church.

In the twentieth century, and especially since Vatican II, the nature of infallibility has come up for very serious reexamination within the Catholic Church. Everyone is now aware of the difficulty of pinning down the exact meaning of religious statements, and of the ways in which words change their meanings according to the cultural situation and point of view of the reader. We are aware, likewise, that the truth of the Gospel is never definitively given, but that it must be won anew through continual efforts to reread the Gospel with the help of the "signs of the times." The doctrine of infallibility seems to suggest that the statements of previous generations can be definitive and adequate, so that we would be dispensed from further inquiry.

These objections do not show that the teaching of Vatican I on infallibility is untenable, but rather that it demands a sophisticated interpretation, according to the methods of modern hermeneutics. As previously mentioned, such reinterpretation is encouraged by the Congregation for the Doctrine of the Faith in its 1973 Declaration, *Mysterium ecclesiae.*[26] Even infallible statements do not escape the limitations inherent in all human speech. Dogmatic statements, insofar as they bear upon the divine, contain an element of special obscurity. The formulations of faith necessarily fall short of capturing the full richness of the transcendent realities to which they refer. Furthermore, as already stated, dogmatic pronouncements are inevitably influenced by the presuppositions, concerns and thought-categories of those who utter them, as well as by the limitations in the available vocabulary. Without contradicting Vatican I's teaching on infallibility, therefore, one may admit that all papal and conciliar dogmas, including the dogma of papal infallibility, are subject to ongoing reinterpretation in the Church.

There remains the problem of how the pope can be infallible by himself, independent of the consent of the Church. Vatican I, in asserting this, was rejecting the Gallican view that papal teaching did not become irreformable until it had been juridically approved by the national hierarchies. This view was seen by Manning and others as imperiling the independence of the Church over national parliaments and kings. Vatican I, however, had no intention of cutting the pope off from the rest of the Church. Indeed, it stated that his infallibility is nothing other than that with which Christ had been pleased to endow the *Church*.

Vatican II, operating in a different historical context,

sought to bring papal infallibility into a positive, organic relationship with the infallibility of the whole Church in believing
and that of the universal pastorate in teaching.[27] In this new
perspective it becomes unthinkable that the pope could infallibly teach anything contrary to the faith of the Church or the
general teaching of the bishops. In the words of *Lumen gentium*: "To the resultant definitions the assent of the Church can
never be wanting, on account of the activity of that same Holy
Spirit, whereby the whole flock of Christ is preserved and pro-
gresses in unity of faith."[28] According to the *relatio* of the
Theological Commission on this passage, infallible definitions
of popes and councils "carry with them and express the consensus of the whole community."[29]

It would not be correct to regard the pope as a mere
mouthpiece for voicing what had previously been agreed to by
the whole Church. As supreme pastor and doctor he has a
special responsibility and charism to teach. But, for the reasons
given above, it seems evident that definitions, if they authenti-
cally flow from the charism of the papal office (which is to
express the faith committed to the whole Church, rather than
the pope's personal convictions), will find an echo in the ranks
of the faithful and will therefore, at least eventually, win assent. If in a given instance the assent of the Church were evi-
dently not forthcoming, this could be interpreted as a signal
that the pope had perhaps exceeded his competence and that
some necessary condition for an infallible act had not been fulfilled.

Understood in this way, there is nothing magical about
papal teaching power. In order to teach infallibly the pope
must align himself with the faith of the whole Church—a faith
already objectified in Scripture and in the documents of tradition. If he were to separate himself from this faith, which lives
on in the believing community, the pope could well become a
heretic or, to use the harsh term of some Reformers, an antichrist. *Corruptio optimi pessima.*

Many Catholic theologians contend that Divine Providence will never permit the pope to fall into error in making a solemn definition.[30] We may piously believe this to be so, but there is no strict proof. In fact there are several objections. For one thing, it is always dangerous to set limits to what Divine Providence will permit. God has allowed many things to go awry, even in the Church. For instance, there have been uncertainties, over a relatively long span of years, as to who was the legitimate pope. Then again, we cannot lightly set aside the common view of medieval theologians and canonists (down to the time of Albert Pighius, if we may accept the authority of Bellarmine) that it is possible for popes, in their public teaching, to fall into heresy.[31] I do not find this view incompatible with the teaching of Vatican I on papal infallibility, since the Council recognized that the pope's infallibility was limited and conditional.

The moderates at Vatican I managed to get so many restrictions written into the text and the explanations given to it on the Council floor that the celebrated definition of papal infallibility really commits one to very little. Minimalistically, or even strictly, interpreted, it is hardly more than an emphatic assertion that the pope's primacy, as defined in the first three chapters of *Pastor aeternus*, extends also to his teaching power. He is not only the first pastor but also the first teacher in the Church. In view of his special responsibility for the unity of the whole Church in the faith of the apostles, it is antecedently credible that in him the infallibility of the whole Church may come to expression. If this be a generally correct interpretation of the basic meaning of chapter IV of *Pastor aeternus*, that chapter is not likely to be rejected by anyone who accepts papal primacy along the lines we have sought to explain it.

2. Ecumenical Possibilities of the Papacy

Does it seem at all likely that the papacy, at least in some remodeled form, will some day come to be accepted by non-

Roman Catholic Christians? Other contributors to this volume will have to speak to this question from their own confessional points of view. As a Roman Catholic, I can foresee the possibility that there might be an increasing consensus, in the future, that some worldwide office or office-holder might be valuable to symbolize and to safeguard the international unity of the Church as a community in which there is "neither Jew nor Greek."

Even so, however, the pope would not easily be able to act as "pastor and teacher of all Christians."[32] In the course of the centuries, the papacy has become so totally identified with the Roman Catholic tradition that it can hardly serve as a credible organ of ecumenical unity. To acknowledge the papacy as it now exists, or as it might foreseeably be modified, would be tantamount to professing Roman Catholicism. To that extent, the papacy remains a stumbling block. It is hard to see how the pope can become more than "pastor and teacher of all Catholics."

Yet one hesitates to conclude that the tragic heritage of past dissension can never be overcome. Perhaps steps can be suggested that might, in some future generation, lead to a Christian union under some kind of papacy. Such an achievement would require a number of preliminary steps both by Roman Catholics and by other Christians.

From the Roman Catholic side, the papal office would have to be reconstructed in such a way that it would cease to bear traces of the imperial or royal absolutism of bygone centuries. Recent Roman Catholic speculations on the primacy of jurisdiction and infallibility, as indicated earlier, tend to show how papal absolutism can be overcome. They suggest how the pope could operate in a more collegial manner, in closer contact with the other pastors and faithful. Other improvements in the papal "style" have been proposed. Some have suggested that the pope should divest himself of responsibility for the ordinary, day-to-day operations of ecclesiastical government and thus liberate himself to play a more inspirational role. Anthony

Spencer[33] and Paul Misner,[34] for example, recommend that the pope should adopt an "affective" behavioral mode, seeking to clarify the purposes of the organization rather than to run the ecclesiastical machine. Andrew Greeley, in a similar vein, argues for a papacy that is predominantly symbolic and interpretive, and for this reason, he declares, more powerful than one that would be purely administrative. "The papacy," he contends, "is not merely an essential sacred symbol for the Christian Church; it also is or at least can be an extraordinarily important institution for facilitating the proclamation of the Gospel and for speaking to the conscience of the world from the Christian perspective."[35] It is easy to imagine that a charismatic papacy, such as Greeley projects, might assume genuinely ecumenical significance.

If the popes of the future are to be taken seriously as speaking to and for all Christians, they will have to have more regular contact with non-Roman Catholics. There will have to be at the Vatican effective ways in which Christians of other traditions can gain access to the pope and assure themselves that consideration is being given to their insights and concerns. The quasi-diplomatic offices of the Secretariat for Promoting Christian Unity, although very useful in their own way, cannot bear the full burden of this task. Other Christian bodies could have regular input into the workings of the Roman Congregations and, in the course of time, could perhaps be given a direct voice in the election of the pope.

At the same time, the pope will have to remain the head of the Roman Catholic communion—a capacity in which he is not likely to be replaced by any other person or agency. He would therefore see to it that his ecumenical functions do not compromise his status as head of the Catholic Church. This fact will make it difficult for non-Roman Catholics to look to him as their spiritual head.

For this reason, it is especially important that the pope should from time to time speak and act conjointly with other spiritual leaders. Under John XXIII and Paul VI, the manifestations of solidarity between the pope and the Patriarch of Constantinople, the pope and the Coptic Patriarch, the pope and the Archbishop of Canterbury, have done much to invest the papacy with an import that transcends confessional differences. The occasional joint undertakings of the Holy See and the World Council of Churches have a similar significance, although they are marred by a certain lack of parallelism between the Catholic Church, which is a confessional body, and the World Council, which is not.

If there is to be any significant growing together, the other Christian communions will have to make a positive contribution. They might consider whether they might take more seriously than in the past what we have called the "Petrine function." Many of them, to all appearances, are content to be churches of particular national or cultural groups. This is unobjectionable provided they also recognize, as is increasingly the case, that the Church of Christ is catholic (in the sense of universal). Regional churches should be encouraged to look upon themselves as partial realizations of a Church that knows no national or ethnic boundaries. They must reactivate their concern for the dimension of catholicity so that the Church may in truth become, in the words of the Uppsala Assembly of the World Council, "the sign of the coming unity of mankind."[36]

While the Roman Catholic Church has at times been excessively centralized, certain other world confessional families presently feel a need to strengthen their universal structures so as to become better signs and instruments of the unity of all in Christ. If this trend continues, they may become organizationally similiar to the Roman Catholic communion of the future. They may seek to introduce into their churches a symbolic focus of worldwide unity, such as the Archbishop of Canterbury has never ceased to be for the Anglican Communion.

If on certain occasions the heads of these other communions were to act in concert with the bishop of Rome, it might be possible to provide for a larger proportion of the Christian faithful the kind of unified pastoral leadership that has been one of the main benefits of the papal office. Such occasional acts of joint leadership would not in themselves be sufficient to provide a "pastor and teacher of all Christians." They would, however, be tokens of the day when all Christians might be visibly gathered under a single spiritual head who would perform for the Church of the future what Peter, according to certain Gospel texts, was chosen to do for the Church of the first generation.

NOTES

1. See G. Thils, *Histoire doctrinale du mouvement oecuménique* (nouvelle édition. Louvain: Warny, 1963), pp. 133, 205.
2. For indications of the background see G.H. Williams, *"Omnium christianorum pastor et doctor*: Vatican I et l'Angleterre victorienne," *Nouvelle revue théologique* 96 (Feb.-Apr. 1974) 113-46, 337-65; V. Conzemius, "Why Was the Primacy of the Pope Defined in 1870?" *Concilium* 91 (The Church as Institution), 75-83; D. Warwick, "The Centralization of Ecclesiastical Authority: An Organizational Perspective," *ibid.*, pp. 109-18.
3. J. H. Newman, *Apologia pro vita sua* (New York: Longmans, Greene, 1905), p. 205. The entire passage from which this quotation is taken provides a splendid illustration of the mentality I am here seeking to describe.
4. C. Davis, "Questions for the Papacy Today," *Concilium* 64 (Papal *Ministry in the Church*), p. 12.
5. G. Thils, *La Primauté pontificale. La doctrine de Vatican I. Les voies d'une révision* (Gembloux: Duculot, 1972). See also his article "The Theology of the Primacy: Towards a Revision," *One in Christ* 10/1 (1974), 13-30.
6. "Declaration in Defense of the Catholic Doctrine on the Church," *Catholic Mind* 71 (Oct. 1973), 54-64, esp. section 5, 58-60. The principles of Section 5 stand on their own merits even though some commentators have pointed out that other sections of *Mysterium Ecclesiae* do not utilize these principles to the best advantage.
7. See A. C. Piepkorn, *"Ius Divinum* and *Adiaphoron* in Relation to Structural Problems in the Church: The Position of the Lutheran Symbolical Books," in P. C. Empie and T. A. Murphy (eds.), *Papal Primacy and the Universal Church* (*Lutherans and Catholics in Dialogue 5*) (Minneapolis: Augsburg, 1974), pp. 119-27; G. A. Lindbeck, "Papal Primacy and *Ius Divinum*: A Lutheran View," *ibid.*, pp. 193-208; C. J. Peter, "Dimensions of

Jus Divinum in Roman Catholic Theology," *Theological Studies* 34/2 (June 1973) 227-50.

8. R. Pesch, "The Position and Significance of Peter in the Church of the New Testament," *Concilium* 64 (*op. cit.*), 21-35; R. E. Brown, K. P. Donfried, and J. Reumann (eds.), *Peter in the New Testament* (Minneapolis: Augsburg and New York: Paulist, 1973).

9. See J. F. McCue, "Roman Primacy in the First Three Centuries," *Concilium* 64 (*op. cit.*), pp. 36-44; *idem*, "The Roman Primacy in the Patristic Era: The Beginnings Through Nicea," in *Papal Primacy and the Universal Church* (*op. cit.*), pp. 44-72.

10. "The Gospel and the Church" (Report of the Joint Lutheran-Roman Catholic Study Commission), *Lutheran World* 19 (1972) 259-73, par. 31; "Differing Attitudes Toward Papal Primacy" (Report to the U.S. Lutheran-Roman Catholic Dialogue,) *Origins* 3/38 (Mar. 14, 1974), nos. 30, 42, and 50.

11. In this chapter this key term will be used in a sense slightly broader than in "Differing Attitudes Toward Papal Primacy," no. 4.

12. I. Salaverri, *De Ecclesia* in *Sacrae Theologiae Summa* (Madrid: Biblioteca de Autores cristianos, 1952), no. 441-42, p. 634.

13. J. D. Mansi (ed.), *Sacrorum Conciliorum nova et amplissima collectio* 52 (Arnhem and Leipzig: Welter, 1927), col. 720.

14. Denzinger-Schönmetzer, *Enchiridion symbolorum* (32nd ed., Freiburg: Herder, 1963) (hereafter cited *DS*), no. 3055.

15. *DS* 3059-64; cf. Salaverri, *op. cit.*, p. 638.

16. Cf. H. Marot, "Unité de l'Eglise et diversité géographique aux premiers siècles," in *L'Episcopat et l'Eglise universelle* (Paris: Cerf, 1962), pp. 565-66.

17. Mansi (*op. cit.*), vol. 52, col. 683B.

18. *Collectio Lacensis* 7 (Freiburg, 1890), pp. 350-51.

19. C. Ernst, "The Primacy of Peter: Theology and Ideology," *New Blackfriars* 50 (1969) 347-55, 399-404.

20. *Ibid.*, p. 403.

21. P. Duprey, "Brief Reflections on the Title 'Primus Inter Pares,'" *One in Christ* 10/1 (1974) 7-12.

22. *Lumen gentium* no. 13; translation in W. M. Abbott, *Documents of Vatican II* (New York: America Press, 1966), p. 32.

23. *DS* 3074.

24. Cf. the Gallican Four Articles of 1682; *DS* 2284.

25. *DS* 3074.

26. Cited above, note 6.

27. *Lumen gentium*, nos. 12 and 25; Abbott, *Documents*, pp. 29-30.

28. *Lumen gentium*, no. 25; Abbott, *Documents*, p. 49. Vatican II is here practically quoting Gasser's famous *relatio* on papal infallibility at Vatican I (Mansi, *op. cit.*, vol. 52, cols. 1213-14). For the interpretation see T. A. Caffrey, "Consensus and Infallibility: The Mind of Vatican I," *Downside Review* 88 (1970) 107-31.

29. *Schema Constitutionis de Ecclesia* (Vatican City: Typis Polyglottis, 1964), p. 98.

30. Such was the view stated by Bishop Gasser in his *relatio*; see Mansi, *op. cit.*, vol. 52, col. 1214.

31. See H. McSorley, "Some Forgotten Truths About the Petrine Ministry," *Journal of Ecumenical Studies* 11/2 (Spring 1974) 208-37, esp. p. 225.

32. *Pastor aeternus*, chap. 4, *DS* 3074.

33. A. Spencer, "The Future of the Episcopal and Papal Roles," *IDOC International* (May 9, 1970), pp. 63-84, following the terminology of Talcott Parsons.

34. Paul Misner, "Papal Primacy in a Pluriform Polity," *Journal of Ecumenical Studies* 11/2 (Spring 1974), pp. 239-61, esp. pp. 254-55.

35. A. M. Greeley, "Advantages and Drawbacks of a Center of Communications in the Church: Sociological Point of View," *Concilium* 64 (*op. cit.*), pp. 101-14; quotation from p. 101.

36. *The Uppsala Report* (Geneva: World Council of Churches, 1968), p. 17.

A Baptist View
of Authority

C. Brownlow Hastings

Bishop Charles H. Helmsing in an address to a Catholic-Baptist Dialogue at Wake Forest University in 1973 was reminiscing about a conversation he once had with a notable Southern Baptist of his Kansas City diocese. President Truman was commenting at the table about his well-known penchant for an occasional social drink. The bishop recalled, "He referred to this at our conversation, and said to me, 'You know, the Baptists threatened to excommunicate me, but they couldn't. The only ones who could excommunicate me were my own congregation, and they wouldn't.' I learned then how Baptists understand *koinonia*, or fellowship, or community, or the local church better than if I had listened to a long lecture on the subject." The conversation turned later to Pope John's recent encyclical, *Pacem in terris*, which Truman warmly praised. The bishop concluded, "All of this made me realize that a Baptist, as a totally dedicated Christian, is formed in social action by free response to the Word of God, by personal meditation and prayer thereon, and by listening to commentaries of others on that Word, whether they be preachers or teachers."[1]

The good bishop has captured the essence of a Baptist view on authority. Baptists share with other Reformation descendants the primacy of the Scriptures as the external authority. They have a unique way of basing the inner light of the

Spirit upon "the competency of the soul in religion" as the internal authority. And they are more willing today than ever to admit that such twofold authority operates within the arena of a fellowship of believers, whether that be defined as "what Baptists have historically believed" or "what I have always been told."

While the arena may condition the operation of authority, it can never be acknowledged as authoritative. While the inner light of the Spirit is essential to the understanding of the revelation God gives to man, such can never be reduced to an individualism or a mysticism that treats lightly God's revelation in history or ignores those who have a like spiritual endowment. While the Scriptures are the "final rule of faith and practice," they are only the means to the end of bringing the believer under the supreme Lordship of Christ.

This is what Bernard Ramm calls a "pattern of authority":

> 1. *Christ*, who is the living, personal Word of God, the supreme revelation of God, the supreme depository of the knowledge of God (Col. 2:3).
> 2. *The Holy Spirit*, who conveys revelation, who delegates its authority, and who witnesses to its divinity.
> 3. *The Sacred Scriptures*, which are inspired by the Holy Spirit and therefore the document of revelation, which witness supremely to Jesus Christ, and which are the Spirit's instrument in effecting illumination.[2]

It will be the thesis of this chapter, therefore, that the Baptist pattern of authority is dynamic and functional rather than static and abstract. While agreeing about the general pattern, Baptists will continue to disagree among themselves over the specifics of the pattern. According to changing pressures both from within and without the Baptist fellowship, they may now stress one or another pole of the pattern. Faced with any claims of hierarchical authority, they will emphasize the immediacy of their access to God through Christ alone. Confronted with critical doubts about the authenticity of the Bible, they may only take deeper refuge in "The Bible says," oblivious to any charge of circular reasoning. When asked by some to accept any list of "fundamentals of faith" as the touchstone of authority, they are likely to remind their overanxious brethren that "confessions are only guides in interpretation, having no authority over the conscience . . . and are not to be used to hamper freedom of thought or investigation in other realms of life."[3] (The viewpoint of this writer is from the position of one who has served his entire ministry within the fellowship of the Southern Baptist Convention. At no point should his remarks be taken as critical of other Baptist groups, nor does his ignorance of their writings intend any slight.)

This kind of functional approach to authority is well illustrated by an experience of the writer. The deacons were painting the parsonage, when he overheard one complaining to his partner of his stomach ailment. "You might heed Paul's injunction and take a little wine for your stomach's sake," encouraged his partner.

Seeing an opportunity to show off his newfound learning in graduate seminary, the young pastor observed, "Brother White, did you know that verse is not in the oldest and best manuscripts of the New Testament?"

"It's in the oldest and best I got!" And he never missed a stroke of the brush. Deacon White's authority was functioning in a very practical way.

Another distinctive feature of this pattern of authority has to do with its locus of concern. Whereas most systems of authority have to do with *certitude* of the truths of religion, most Baptists are concerned with *assurance* in the experience of religion. Not, how can I be certain I am right, but, how can I be assured I am saved? This does not mean that the Baptist is unconcerned about the pursuit of truth. But suspicious of all claims by men, whether pope or scholar, church or philosophy, to encompass all of God's truth, he is content to order his priorities more modestly: "The Spirit himself beareth witness with our spirit, that we are children of God" (Rom. 8:16; all Scripture quotations are from the American Standard Version, 1901). Because of this inner witness he responds warmly to Paul's "for I know him whom I have believed, and I am persuaded that he is able to guard that which I have committed unto him against that day" (2 Tim. 1:12). While he may agree fully with the truths of the Niceno-Constantinoplian Creed, he is unmoved over a *filioque* debate, since he already has experienced the Son, who is "the way, the truth, and the life."

Now there is nothing distinctive about the *fact* of the Lordship of Christ. Practically all Christians agree to the fact. It is the *way* that Lordship operates for the believer that makes the Baptist view unique. Ideally the Lordship of Christ is given as full and complete freedom to operate over the individual conscience as human frailty will permit. Every safeguard is taken to allow it to be undelegated, direct, experiential. In the final moment of decision, which may even be taken in concert with other believers, the soul stands naked before its Lord and cries, "What shall *I* do, Lord?" (Acts 22:10).

The very fact that the believer asks the question indicates that he is not deriving his authority from his reason or his conscience. It saves him from arrogant subjectivism. In finding the answer, however, the total man is involved: reason and conscience, memory and understanding, human wisdom and spiritual insight.

Now the average believer in the heat of decision-making is not all this analytical, but if he were, his reasoning might proceed something like this. "God, having of old time spoken unto the fathers in the prophets by divers portions and in divers manners, hath at the end of these days spoken unto us in his Son" (Heb. 1:1-2). "And the Word became flesh, and dwelt among us. . . . No man hath seen God at any time; the only-begotten Son, who is in the bosom of the Father, he hath declared him" (John 1:14, 18). Now the New Testament is a faithful record of those who were "eyewitnesses and ministers of the word" (Luke 1:2). As "inspired of God [it is] also profit-able for teaching, for reproof, for correction, for instruction which is in righteousness: that the man of God may be com-plete, furnished completely unto every good work" (2 Tim. 3:16-17).

If he is mature and well-taught he will draw upon the un-derstandings of the Scriptures both from those who have gone on before and those teachers in whom he has confidence. And Baptists perhaps more than any other major denomination have emphasized continuing Bible study for adults. It often seems like an end in itself or a flight into the first century, but it is ultimately directed toward that moment of truth when the soul needs to answer: "What shall *I* do, Lord?"

But he does not stop there, even with the finest interpreta-tion of the Scriptures. He knows that as a believer under the New Covenant he has a promise that supersedes all claims to sacerdotal power: "I will put my laws into their mind, and on their heart also will I write them. . . . And they shall not teach every man his fellow-citizen, and every man his brother, saying, Know the Lord: For all shall know me, from the least to the greatest of them" (Heb. 8:10-11). He does not despise the gift of teaching, but he surrenders his mind and conscience to no teacher, pastor or friend, for he knows that he has the same open Bible and the same indwelling Spirit to give him light as they do. "And as for you, the anointing which ye received of him abideth in you, and ye need not that any one teach you; but as his anointing teacheth you concerning all things, and is true, and is no lie, and even as it taught you, ye abide in him" (1 John 2:27; even concatenating Scripture refer-ences is characteristic of his style of reasoning; such is a very ancient method, going back to the lectionaries of the first Christian centuries).

This "competency of the soul," as E. Y. Mullins has called it in *The Axioms of Religion*, is not a natural self-suf-ficiency, nor an arrogant individualism. It is a divine gift to all men everywhere by virtue of their being made in the image of

God. It corresponds somewhat to the idea of natural grace as expounded by Catholic theologians. It is the ability of man to respond to the movement of the Spirit of God. It is not destroyed by sin nor restored by baptism. It is the *sine qua non* of God's dealing directly with every sort of man, no matter what his human condition of sin and ignorance may be.

To this competency of the soul there is added then the continuing presence of the Spirit of Christ, who claims possession of the believer upon his free and intelligent commitment to Jesus as Lord. This presence may be masked or ignored by the unfaithful believer, but it can never be lost or destroyed. The *sense* of the Spirit's presence can be heightened in worship, in fellowship with other believers, in prayer or in human crises, but the *reality* does not change.

This is the reason few Baptists can get worked up over being denied communion by Roman Catholics, Orthodox and certain others. Holding that the bread and the wine are symbols and not efficient means of conveying the presence of Christ, they do not feel deprived, for they not only have the presence within but they sense his presence in their fellow believers, whatever their theology may be.

Baptists, therefore, read each individual's privileges in the light of the New Covenant and the abiding presence of the Spirit. Believers are "sons of God" (Rom. 8:14), a "kingdom and priests" (Rev. 1:6), the "people of God" (1 Pet. 2:10). Since this is so, then all ecclesial structure must safeguard this freedom and nurture these privileges. Therefore, ecclesial authority is confined to the local church, which as the prime association of believers has the ultimate responsibility to each individual. Believers then associate together on the basis of a "church covenant." This is not a creed, which binds belief upon pain of excommunication. Nor is it a "confession of faith" which "constitutes a consensus of opinion of some Baptist body, large or small, for the general instruction and guidance of our own people and others concerning those articles of the Christian faith which are most surely held among us."[4] It is simply a pledge to support one another and the ministries of the church with Christian conduct and love.

Claude Broach has stated the implications of local church authority and autonomy:

This group of believers acts freely, without constraint or supervision from any human authority, to order and govern its own life according to the New Testament. All decisions are made by vote of the congregation, with every member having equal standing and responsibility before God. Here are some of the things the local congregation must decide for itself:
—whom it wishes to ordain to the ministry;
—whom it wishes to choose as its pastor;
—whom it will elect as its deacons;
—how to operate its church school and total program of religious education;
—how to raise and disperse funds;
—how it will receive and care for its members;
—the order of service followed in public worship;
—committee structure to strengthen parish life and encourage participation in Christian service;
—extent of cooperation with other Baptist and Christian groups.[5]

It might be added that authority to administer "the ordinances"—baptism and the Lord's Supper—is not automatically conferred by the laying on of hands in ordination. It is reserved to the wish of the congregation and may be delegated to any member or even to a visiting minister. Ordination, then, is the corporate act of the congregation, whereby they recognize the evidences of the gifts and calling of God to a peculiar ministry and "set apart" such a one publicly for that end.

Consequent to the principle of local church authority and autonomy, Baptists do not delegate any powers beyond the congregation. There is no such thing as "The Southern Baptist

Church" beyond the Jones Street Baptist Church or the First
Baptist Church of Anywhere. They can say, "The New Testament speaks also of the church as the body of Christ which
includes all of the redeemed of all ages,"[6] but they do not conceive of its institutional expression beyond the local church.
Consequently, Baptist associations, the first level of cooperation in missions, education, and benevolent work, state conventions, the Southern Baptist Convention and the Baptist World
Alliance, are all made up of "messengers" from local churches,
who constitute themselves an autonomous body for the purpose
of carrying on ministries too difficult for a local congregation.
There is no such thing as a Baptist "judicatory," as Truman
pointed out. Most Baptists would not even relate the word
ecclesially.

By and large Baptists have never been greatly impressed
with the claims for or the search for a "true church." Most
such movements, as for example, Landmarkism, which arose in
the nineteenth century and held to a kind of "baptismal succession" as the sign of the true church, have proved either divisive
or inconsequential. Holding that the only conceptual "church"
he has to deal with is the First Baptist Church on the square or
the Jones Street Baptist Church, he is more aware of its human
composition than of its divine nature. Its fellowship, ministries
and worship are no less available to his highest dedication than
to those whose Church is the means of their salvation or the
continuing incarnation of their Lord. He is much more concerned with whether and how his church and denomination are
carrying out the Great Commission than whether his local
church is in all respects truly apostolic, holy, one and universal.
His criteria are, therefore, very pragmatic: Is this particular
church preaching the Bible? Are souls being saved? Is the fellowship warm and satisfying? What can they do for my children? Are they mission-minded? In this mobile age, if the answers to too many of these questions are weak or negative, he
is not too disturbed, for he can always keep moving his affiliation.

So far we have approached a Baptist view of authority from the functional and practical standpoint. What do the theologians have to say?

Baptists have an inherited distrust of human reason, even reasoning about their faith. There is the anecdote about the preacher who took two hours with a highly reasoned sermon on the Proofs of the Existence of God. At the door one of his more pious members remonstrated: "Parson, in spite of your sermon I still believe in God!" She was enunciating a deep-ingrained feeling among Baptists: that the heart has its reasons one's mind can but dimly grasp. This does not mean that one reasons as far as he can, then takes a leap of faith into knowledge which is "out there in the dim unknown." Nor does it mean that faith is necessarily opposed to reason. It simply means in the mind of such humble believers that faith, which is more personal trust in the Lord than assent to a body of beliefs, is a more reliable way of knowing ultimate reality than is reason. To label this as "fideism" or "believerism" is to slander the witness of those who have experienced its end result: "peace with God through our Lord Jesus Christ" (Rom. 5:1). Their prayer for all men would be, "Now the God of hope fill you with all joy and peace in believing, that ye may abound in hope, in the power of the Holy Spirit" (Rom. 15:13).

Let us review briefly Baptist confessions of faith, with the limitations to these already pointed out. One of the earliest, which represents the thinking of the two groups of English Separatists in London and Amsterdam, out of which the earliest Baptists arose, is *A True Confession* drawn up in 1595. Article 7 reads as follows:

7. That the rule of this knowledge faith and obedience, concerning the worship and service of God and all other Christian duties, is not the opinions, devises, laws or constitutions of men, but the written word of the everlasting God, contained in the canonical books of the Old and New Testaments.[7]

One of the most complete statements of the authority of the Scriptures and of the need for inner illumination of the Spirit came from the London conference in 1689 of one hundred and seven Baptist churches. This *Second London Confession* was a rewriting of one originally issued in 1677 by a group of Baptists to show their general concurrence with the famous Westminster Confession of 1646 (out of the Calvinist churches of England). It begins a long chapter on the Scriptures thus:

1. The Holy Scripture is the only sufficient, certain, and infallible rule of all saving Knowledge, Faith, and Obedience; although the light of Nature, and the works of Creation and Providence do so far manifest the goodness, wisdom and power of God, as to leave men unexcusable; yet they are not sufficient to give that knowledge of God and His will, which is necessary unto Salvation. . . .[8]

The two most widely used confessions of faith in the last two hundred years have been the Philadelphia Confession of 1742 and the New Hampshire Confession of 1833. The wording of the New Hampshire Confession is practically unchanged in that adopted by the Southern Baptist Convention in 1925 and again in 1963:

We believe the Holy Bible was written by men divinely inspired, and is a perfect treasure of heavenly instruction; that it has God for its author, salvation for its end, and truth, without any mixture of error, for its matter; that it reveals the principles by which God will judge us; and therefore is, and shall remain to the end of the world, the true center of Christian union, and the supreme standard by which all human conduct, creeds and opinions should be tried.[9]

While not exactly a confession of faith, a pamphlet entitled "Baptist Ideals" published by the Sunday School Board of the Southern Baptist Convention and drawn up in 1974 by a committee of eighteen, Ralph A. Herring, chairman, describes the threefold pattern of authority. Its summary statements are as follows:

1. Christ as Lord. The ultimate source of authority is Jesus Christ the Lord, and every area of life is to be subject to his lordship.

2. The Scriptures. The Bible as the inspired revelation of God's will and way, made full and complete in the life and teachings of Jesus Christ, is our authoritative rule of faith and practice.

3. The Holy Spirit. The Holy Spirit is God actively revealing himself and his will to man. He therefore interprets and confirms the voice of divine authority.

The ultimate unity and direction of movement of this pattern of authority is expressed in the closing paragraph on the Spirit: "The Spirit seeks to achieve God's will and purpose among men. He empowers Christians for the work of ministry and sanctifies and preserves the redeemed for the praise of Christ. He calls for a free and dynamic response to the Lordship of Christ and for a creative and faithful obedience to the Word of God."

From this can be seen the writer's emphasis that a Baptist view of authority is dynamic and functional. Nowhere is the end result seen as true or orthodox doctrines or beliefs, the true church, a rule or deposit of faith, or an infallible agent or agency. The moral and spiritual goal of submission to the Lordship of Christ, while always imperfectly realized under the human predicament, is obtainable practically without the agony of establishing finally those historical ecclesial issues.

Let us turn to some representative theologians of the twentieth century for their Baptist views on authority. One of the few major voices writing a full monograph on the subject was that of E. Y. Mullins, President of Southern Baptist Theological Seminary, Louisville, during the years 1899-1928. His book, *The Axioms of Religion* (1908), is still a classic exposition of the distinctive Baptist beliefs. His major opus, *The Christian Religion in Its Doctrinal Expression* (1920), served a number of generations of seminarians as the text in philosophy of religion.

Mullins wrote *Freedom and Authority in Religion* as an apologetic at the height of the Modernist controversies that swept all Christian ranks around the turn of the century. His book reflects the polemics with scientific and philosophical thought which tended to deny the supernatural and locate authority in religion, when it was allowed at all, in the feeling or the conscience alone. He wrote in answer to Schleiermacher, Sabatier, Martineau and Oman. His work came out in the same year as P. T. Forsyth's classic on the subject, *The Principle of Authority* (1913).

In *Freedom and Authority* Mullins begins by showing that the modern passion for freedom in all realms needs to be brought under a true authority, when man "wisely and properly seeks to adjust himself to the universe, regarded as physical, social, political, moral or religious."[10]

He denies that religious man is shut up to the alternative of "the authoritative absolutism of the Roman Catholic Church and the absolute individualism on the subjective criterion of truth."[11] This supposedly came about when the thinking Protestant give up his concept of an infallible Bible under the attacks of biblical criticism. Rather his goal is expressed:

> We stand for the free development of human personality, the complete unfolding of all man's powers—intellectual, moral, and spiritual—in short, for the perfection of man. But we hold and shall try to show that this end is to be achieved not by the abolition of the principle of authority, but by its recognition.[12]

While Mullins held equally to the Christian revelation as both subjective and objective, under the polemics of the time he sought to restore a balance by rehabilitating the objective and by pointing out the dangers of subjectivism. It is in this context that he may surprise our readers with his attack on "Symbolo-Fideism." An authority based upon an inner core of faith that can only be expressed in indeterminate symbols is beyond the reach of theological debate.

It is because of this context also that we find his definition of authority using "external":

> . . . we may for the present define authority as any external expression of reality or truth or power which is indispensable and binding, which we cannot escape, which is inevitable for us, which environs us so that to escape it we must change the nature of reality itself, or else pursue a course which will destroy ourselves.[13]

There is a proper place for creeds, he says, as an expression of understanding of the Christian faith, a means of defense against attack, "for purposes of Christian unity and as a means of propagating the faith."[14] No external authority has the right to deny the free formulation of creeds and confessions, but:

> It is equally true, however, that the imposition of creeds by authority is also a form of tyranny to be resisted. . . . The peril of creeds is in the tendency to substitute them for life. They become barriers to the free development of personality in religion whenever the holding of them as true, and the propagation of them as mere intellectual beliefs take the place of the free intercourse of God and man in religion.[15]

In approaching the place of the Bible in Christianity Mullins will not call it a final authority, for he has given that preeminence already to Christ. The Bible is to be used as "an authority in religion just insofar as it is the source whence we derive truth as to man's relations with God."[16] He stresses the interdependence of the literature and the life. First came the divine action and the human interaction in the revelation, then the literature. The Bible finds its unity in Christ. There is a progressive revelation of God through the Old Testament that finds its completion in Christ. Then the life under the guidance of the Spirit produced the literature, which is necessary for its continued nourishment. The literature preserves the eyewitness account of the final and complete revelation. Were it not for that, human traditions would so change the revelation as to make necessary periodically a fresh incarnation to restore its purity.

To those who object that this is thrusting a book between the soul and God, Mullins claims that such a complaint would sever the literature from the life which the Spirit develops in its use among men. "Scripture then is not a veil, but a rent in the veil between man and God, for its function is to lead to Christ."[17] The astronomer is not accused of worshiping his telescope nor expected to study the stars *de nouveau*.

On the problem of the formation of the canon he identifies two factors at work in the early church long before any formal council passed judgment: the weight of apostolic eyewitness and the spiritual affinity of the life within the early community to those particular books and no others. The very fact that the early church found it necessary under pressure of such criticism as that of Marcion or such subjectivism as the Montanists indicated that there was a need to draw a line as close to the origin as feasible.

How, then, are we to consider the Bible as authority?

The reply is that its finality as authority is due to its unique power of showing the way without compelling man; or rather its capacity for revealing destiny and then of constraining man to it; or yet again, its disclosure of the inner constitution of the moral and spiritual universe, while leaving man free to conform to it. It is not state or rule or decree; it is a moral and spiritual constitution. The Bible is the revelation of the constitution of the personal kingdom which includes God and man.[18]

Among contemporary theologians, Dale Moody, professor of theology, Southern Baptist Theological Seminary, Louisville, has said, "The seat of authority in Christian faith is Christ. . . . Any claim to ecclesiastical authority apart from the Christ of the Scriptures and the Holy Spirit degenerates into religious despotism."[19] In an address to the Baptist-Catholic Dialogue at Wake Forest in 1973, Moody included with the above statements the role of the church. It is "to be the body of Christ and to bear witness to the Head who is Christ. All who are in Christ are in the body of Christ, and no denomination or any other group of members has the right to say they alone constitute the body of Christ. The body is to manifest the manifold wisdom of God, not to magnify her own authority and rights in the world (Eph. 3:10)."[20]

At another Baptist-Catholic Dialogue at Wake Forest, 1974, E. Glenn Hinson, professor of church history at Southern Baptist Seminary, dealt very honestly with the influence of tradition in Baptist life on the matter of authority. He found the "definitive authority" in religion to be in the revelation itself, finding some sympathetic response to Vatican II in its *Dogmatic Constitution on Divine Revelation.* He would even allow a "Baptist magisterium" so long as it is conceived as comprising "the whole body of Christ, including the laity."[21]

Concluding Remarks

It will surprise no one, Baptists least of all, that such a pattern of authority as we have described is susceptible to all kinds of stresses and strains. They will continue to argue among themselves and with the wider Christian community of

scholars over all biblical issues, denominational polity, ecumenical participation, and spiritual movements. There will
always be a conservative tendency to enforce confessions of
faith, or some "fundamentals," as tests of orthodoxy. As
churches and denominations grow and develop highly complex
ministries with great financial outlays, the social forces that
afflict all institutions tempt individuals and groups to short-cir-
cuit the freedoms and the autonomy so long cherished.

Two issues currently reflect the problems of Baptists with
authority. The fundamentalist movement has sought to impose
a theory of inspiration of the Bible based on claims of infallibility, literally interpreted. With their high regard for the
Scriptures Baptists are particularly vulnerable. Hugh Wamble,
professor of history, Midwestern Baptist Theological Seminary, Kansas City, has tried to maintain a balanced view:

> The Scriptures' authority and infallibility relate to its su-
> premacy as a rule for religious faith and practice. The of-
> ficial records of Baptists, prior to the twentieth century,
> do not claim that the Scriptures' authority is dependent
> upon its historical accuracy or that it pertains to non-
> religious areas. There are some individuals, however, who
> assert that none of the Bible can be authoritative unless all
> of it is inerrant. Some self-styled Bible-lovers even suggest
> that it should be thrown away if it has one error. Quite
> frankly, it is hard to understand how anyone could trea-
> sure his theory about the Bible more than the Bible itself.[22]

Some Baptists will continue to insist on the "plenary ver-
bal inspiration" producing an infallible Bible as being the sum
of the Word of God. But even in their own interpretation and
use, they do not carry through to the logical conclusion that
every word is divinely dictated and on the same level of revelation. Clifton J. Allen, editor of *The Broadman Bible Commentary*, in his introductory article, "The Book of the Christian
Faith," has pointed out the untenableness of such extremism:

"Particularly, this view involves the problems of a divine will virtually imposed on the writers of the Scriptures, the submergence of the findings of critical studies as controverting full inspiration, and attributing to God attitudes and actions seemingly out of harmony with his revelation in Christ."[23]

Having rejected all other monistic theories of authority, Baptists by and large are not ready to have even their cherished Scriptures so elevated. They remember the words of Jesus: "Ye search the Scriptures, because ye think that in them ye have eternal life; and these are they which bear witness of me; and ye will not come to me, that ye may have life" (John 5:39-40).

The other issue which has proved very divisive among Baptists is the charismatic movement. It may come as a surprise, since on the one hand Baptists esteem spiritual and pietistic movements generally and on the other the charismatic movement has greatly stressed Bible reading and study. Several factors may enter into their fear. First, with no authoritarian creeds to put fences to define and protect the body of truth, any movement which claims a later revelation than the New Testament is automatically suspect. If revelation is always open in the sense of new and underived truth about God and his relations with man, then there will always be the possibility that some man—pope, Morman, or Muslim—will propose a new revelation on an authority which is above the scrutiny of others. The advantage of a closed revelation is just here, that I, as well as any other lowly believer, have access to the same source of truth with confidence that my competence under the Holy Spirit is adequate to whatever measure of apprehension is necessary for me. It is this egalitarian character of the fellowship of believers that makes any claim to special sanctity or powers a threat. Finally, while ordination does not carry with it any sacerdotal powers for Baptists, it is assumed that the pastor will naturally be the best expression of charismatic leadership in the church. If some member or group claims a higher degree of charisma and seeks to enforce such in a judgmental manner, it will constitute a threat to his leadership and the spirit of unity of the congregation.

By now it should be self-evident that Baptists could never accept the office of the papacy. They value liberty of the soul and the freedom of the Holy Spirit within the fellowship too much to delegate any powers to a man or group of men that would compromise these hard-won consequences of their pattern of authority.

There are two arguments which have been advanced recently for Protestants to accept some kind of modified papacy. Let us look at the first briefly and the second at more length.

1. "Christianity needs a symbolical voice to give expression to the Word of the Lord today." This implies that such a voice has the mind of the Lord without question. It is very easy to demonstrate that there is a great segment of Christendom which is perfectly willing to admit such a need. Baptists would claim for all of them what they claim for themselves, that such a need can be met by each Christian individually and the people of God collectively through the open Bible and the leadership of the Spirit of God within. Furthermore, those who feel no such need will not be influenced by the mere expression of an authoritative voice. Where authority is denied, acceptance must be earned. This is the principle of leadership as over against that of dogmatism.

It is sufficient for Baptists to allow Roman Catholics to continue the debate over "infallibility." They have observed that in 105 years since the dogma was promulgated only once has the power been claimed (1950), and that without justification either from Scripture or early Church Fathers. Other papal decrees are open to endless debate over interpretation and application, as witness the consequences of *Humanae vitae* (1968). And, of course, all agree that there are no such things as degrees of infallibility.

2. "The ministry of primacy is needed as a service to unity in truth and love." The only expression of unity Baptists trust is that which evolves upward from the people of God. Any effort to impose unity downward is always a cause of suspicion and division. Any primacy which is proffered to a leader in actual practice comes from the recognition of the Spirit of

truth and love which is demonstrated convincingly in the life of the one so honored.

What, then, is the nature of the unity which Baptists seek? Historically, they have been burned many times by the well-intentioned efforts at devising a structural unity. This tying of the tops of the hierarchical trees has tended to force conformity upon a people without respect for their pluralism and diversity. It usually is accompanied by loss of freedoms, including the unbiblical linking of church and state. There seems to be no historical justification for the hope that *any* societal power structure, even that which arises out of the Christian Gospel, can avoid the temptation either to dominate other powers or to be compromised by them.

On the other hand, while admitting that they have not been in the forefront of structural ecumenism, most Baptists would see a great future for the kind of functional unity that comes from many groups of Christians working together in missions, evangelism and social service and action. And with no juridical structure themselves, their own record in these fields proves that such a functional unity is possible. It might also be pointed out that with no authoritarian *magisterium* Baptists have maintained a more uniform interpretation of the Gospel than even contemporary Roman Catholicism. It is to be hoped that with maturing relationships and cooperative work with other Christian bodies Baptists will be able to profit by and contribute to the kind of unity of spirit in the midst of diversity by love in action.

Let us look further at the biblical evidence on "the Petrine office." The only primacy Baptists can see in the New Testament for Peter is that of leadership and service, not of authority. Granted that Peter is the "rock" on which Christ builds his church, he shares this foundation role with the other apostles and the prophets (Eph. 2:20), while Jesus himself is the chief cornerstone. Though Peter uses *lithos* rather than *petra*, he uses the same figure of building the spiritual house on Jesus as the "living stone" and all Christians as themselves living stones (1 Pet. 2:4-7).

The role of the apostles is first of all that of eyewitnesses to the resurrection, which cannot be handed on. Karl Rengstorf, in his article on apostleship in the *Theologisches Worterbuch zum Neuen Testament*, finds the closest Hebrew parallel in the word *shaliah*, an agent who "is always the representative of the person who commissions him, and as such exercises his right."[24] The "apostle" can take no initiative beyond what his Lord commands (cf. John 5:19; 20:21). When his mission is complete his commission expires. He cannot delegate it.

There is wider use of "apostle" beyond that of the Twelve. At first it seems the disciples before Pentecost felt the need to maintain the number twelve, and so selected Matthias to fill the role created by the defection of Judas. But there was no such consciousness with reference to the successor of James, the brother of John, at his martyrdom. Since the work of an apostle came to be seen as proclaiming the Gospel, attested by validating signs (2 Cor. 12:12), in new mission fields, others such as Paul, Barnabas and perhaps Andronicus and Junius (Rom 16:7) were called apostles. Certainly no theologian or historian would claim that the later role of bishop as presiding over a geographical entity can be evidenced in apostolic times, even in germ.

The power of binding and loosing given to Peter (Mt. 16:19, only Gospel!) is derived from the rabbinic interpretation of what things are permitted and what are forbidden under the law of Moses. But this same power is given shortly thereafter to all the disciples (Mt. 18:1) with the whole church as the context (Mt. 18:17-18).

The symbol of the "keys of the kingdom" is likewise drawn from Isaiah 22:15-22, where the stewardship of the royal treasurer is taken from him and promised to another. In Revelation 3:7 Jesus claims to have "the key of David" and in Revelation 1:18 "the keys of death and Hades." If this is seen as the power of admitting or denying entrance to the Kingdom, Peter had much to learn before he could see God admitting Gentiles (Acts 10 and 11). Paul says such revelation was given to all the apostles and prophets (Eph. 3:4-6). At the Council of

Jerusalem (Acts 15) Peter reported his experience with Cornelius, but it was James, the "Lord's brother," who presided and made the suggestion which was adopted by "the apostles and elders with the whole church" (Acts 15:22). The Baptist scholar, John A. Broadus, says: "Peter and the other apostles would admit or deny admission, as they would forgive sins or retain them, by teaching the spiritual conditions of admission or forgiveness, and by their inspired power of discerning and declaring a man's spiritual condition."[25]

Peter's leadership is readily granted among the disciples, but it was no more authoritative than any leadership which can be explained by personality, "charisma" and human opportunism.[26]

The command of the Lord to Peter in Galilee after the resurrection to "feed my sheep" carries no special function for Peter alone. The role of "feeding" (John 21:17) is a far cry from authoritarian disciplines. The "pastoring" function (John 21:16) belongs to all those called and commissioned of the Lord (Acts 20:28, the elders of the church at Ephesus; Eph. 4:11, where "pastors and teachers" are distinct from apostles and prophets). This is the only "Petrine office" which is acknowledged by Baptists. Peter himself renounced an authoritarian role over his "fellow-elders": "neither as lording it over the charge allotted to you, but making yourselves examples to the flock" (1 Pet. 5:1-3). Any authoritarian control over the people of God, therefore, denies the duality of the same Spirit dwelling in both pastor and sheep, and so denies the latter's competency under God. It also denies the principle of leadership the Lord gave to his apostles: "The kings of the Gentiles have lordship over them; and they that have authority over them are called Benefactors. But ye shall not be so: but he that is the greater among you, let him become as the younger, and he that is chief, as he that doth serve" (Luke 22:25-26).[27]

For these reasons Baptists cannot recognize primacy of person or office in any man as claimed for the papacy nor surrender autonomy to any ecclesial body beyond that of the immediate congregation of the people of God.

The goal of religious authority as stated by E. Y. Mullins is worth repeating: "We stand for the free development of human personality, the complete unfolding of all man's power —intellectual, moral and spiritual—in short, for the perfection of man." Baptists believe that the final revelation of God which we have in Jesus Christ is available to all men who may base their adventures of exploration safely there, for such is not the privileged possession of savants, scientists or sacerdotalists.

In closing his commentary on Jeremiah the writer has spoken of what it means to live under that "new covenant" the prophet foretold:

> The church, then, is a fellowship of those who have a common experience—the forgiveness of sins; a common Master—who mediates the new covenant, which we commemorate at every Lord's Supper; a common Spirit— "who will guide you into all the truth." These are the only valid reasons for a church having a congregational form of polity and operating on a democratic basis. Not that the majority is always right, not that *vox populi* is always *vox Dei*. But that the congregational polity is the only human guarantee that the Spirit of God has the freedom to speak the mind of God to the people of God. . . .

> Here then is true freedom: from the tyranny of external authority, from the chains of a conscience that cannot forgive itself, from the fear of an unpredictable God. Here is the heart of true religion: not in a sacrificial system that leads nowhere but to frustration; not in pietism that ultimately leads to pharisaism; not in perfectionism that is the final form of selfishness. It is rather to be found simply in becoming "my people"—to be what he wants, to go where he sends, to do what he says—and to rejoice in nothing more and nothing less than that he is "my God."[28]

NOTES

1. J. William Angell, ed., *Catholics and Baptists in Ecumenical Dialogue* (The Ecumenical Institute of Wake Forest University, 1973), pp. 10-11.

2. Bernard Ramm, *The Pattern of Authority* (Grand Rapids: Eerdmans, 1957), p. 36.

3. Preamble to the report of the Committee on Statement of Baptist Faith and Message, adopted by the Southern Baptist Convention, May 9, 1963.

4. *Preamble, loc. cit.*

5. Claude U. Broach, *The Baptists* (New York: Paulist Press, 1967), pp. 16-17.

6. *The Baptist Faith and Message*, Article VI, adopted by the Southern Baptist Convention, 1963.

7. W.L. Lumpkin, *Baptist Confessions of Faith* (Philadelphia: The Judson Press, 1959, p. 84. Used by permission.

8. *Ibid.*, p. 248.

9. *Ibid.*, pp. 361ff. I am indebted for this summary to the address of Dr. J. William Angell, professor of religion, Wake Forest University, to the Baptist-Catholic Dialogue of May 1973, entitled "Baptists and the Authority of the Scriptures."

10. E.Y. Mullins, *Freedom and Authority of Religion* (Philadelphia: The Griffith and Rowland Press, 1913), p. 14.

11. *Ibid.*, p. 31.

12. *Ibid.*, p. 32.

13. *Ibid.*, p. 47.

14. *Ibid.*, p. 301.

15. *Ibid.*, pp. 301-302.

16. *Ibid.*, p. 342

17. *Ibid.*, p. 352.

18. *Ibid.*, pp. 396-397.

19. *Encyclopedia of Southern Baptists*, I, Art. "Authority" (Nashville: Broadman Press, 1958), p. 99.

20. J. William Angell, *op. cit.*, p. 30.

21. *Seminar on Authority* (Wake Forest: The Ecumenical Institute, 1974), p. 62.

22. Hugh Wamble, "Baptists, the Bible and Authority," *Foundations*, July 1963, 6:212.

23. Clifton J. Allen, general ed., *The Broadman Bible Commentary* I (Nashville: Broadman Press), 1969, p. 8.

24. *Bible Key Words* IV, trans. and ed. by J.R. Coates and H.P. Kingdom (New York: Harper and Brothers, 1958), p. 14.

25. John A. Broadus, *An American Commentary on the New Testament*, Art "Matthew" (Philadelphia: American Baptist Publication Society, 1886), p. 361.

26. See Rengstorf, *op. cit.*, p. 49.

27. Cf. the fine argument for this kind of authority of loving service by Fr. John L. McKenzie, *Authority in the Church* (Garden City, N.Y.: Doubleday, 1971).

28. *Advanced Bible Study*, April-May-June 1971. © Copyright 1971 The Sunday School Board of the Southern Baptist Convention. All rights reserved. Used by permission.

Authority in the Reformed Tradition

Ross Mackenzie

Toward the end of April 1538, the General Council commanded Calvin and two of his colleagues to depart from the city of Geneva within three days. The first attempt to reform the city in faith and manners "according to the Word of God" had failed. Accordingly, Cardinal Jacopo Sadoleto, a moderate Catholic reformer of the Erasmian type, composed a letter inviting the disaffected citizens of Geneva to return to their former allegiance:

The point in dispute [the cardinal wrote] is whether it is more expedient for your salvation, and whether you think you will do what is more pleasing to God, by believing and following what the Catholic Church throughout the whole world, now for more than fifteen hundred years, or (if we require clear and certain recorded notice of the facts) for more than thirteen hundred years, approves with general consent; or innovations introduced within these twenty-five years, by crafty, or, as they think themselves, acute men; but men certainly who are not themselves the Catholic Church. For, to define it briefly, the Catholic Church is that which in all parts, as well as at the present time, in every region of the world, united and consenting in Christ, has been always and everywhere directed by the one Spirit of Christ.[1]

94

The letter was a persuasive argument from an urbane apologist who had associated with conciliators such as Lorenzo Campeggio, Reginald Pole, and Gaspar Contarini. It reproduced a commonplace of Catholic apologetic, the dictum of St. Vincent of Lerins: Let us hold that which has been believed everywhere, always, and by all. For Sadoleto as for St. Vincent, the authority of the church to teach was grounded on the principles of *universitas* ("throughout the whole world"), *antiquitas* ("now for more than fifteen hundred years"), and *consensio* ("with general consent").

In his reply, written in a careful and guarded manner, Calvin summarized what he regarded as his opponent's argument:

> The best rule for the due worship of God is that which is prescribed by the church, and that, therefore, there is no salvation for those who have violated the unity of the church unless they repent.

Calvin then dealt with the question of salvation and the "prime motive" of human existence, which is "zeal to illustrate the glory of God." Nothing is more perilous to our salvation than a "preposterous and perverse worship of God." So the question was: Which of the two parties—Reformed or Roman Catholic —retained that worship of God which is alone legitimate? Sadoleto had erred in his understanding of the church:

> When you describe it as that which in all parts, as well as at the present time, in every region of the earth, being united and consenting in Christ, has been always and everywhere directed by the one Spirit of Christ, what comes of the Word of the Lord, that clearest of all marks? . . . For seeing how dangerous it would be to boast of the Spirit without the Word, he declared that the church is indeed governed by the Holy Spirit, but in order that that government might not be vague and unstable, he annexed it to the Word.

"The church is indeed governed by the Holy Spirit, but that government is bound to the Word"—these words constitute Calvin's doctrine of authority in the church. Sadoleto's error, as Calvin understood things, was that he had separated the Spirit from the Word. The Spirit does not lead us into any novelty independent of the gospel. By the Word the church "tests all doctrines." What, then, of Sadoleto's charge that all that the Catholic Church had approved for fifteen hundred years by the uniform consent of the faithful was being torn up and destroyed by the reformers? "Our agreement with antiquity is far closer than yours," Calvin responded. "All we have attempted has been to renew that ancient form of the church." Calvin then enumerated the four things on which the church is founded: doctrine, discipline, the sacraments, and ceremonies (meaning forms of worship, etc.). All the reformers had done was to "restore the native purity" from which these had degenerated. Scholastic theology was far removed from the simplicity commended by Paul, and doctrines like justification by faith had come to be stressed only because the Romanists had impiously effaced it from memory.

Did these differences provide sufficient reason for schism in the holy church? The real reason for the protest of the reformers, Calvin argued, was that "the light of divine truth has been extinguished, the Word of God buried, the virtue of Christ left in profound oblivion, and the pastoral office subverted." Those who contended against such evils were not declaring war against the church. Rather, they assisted it in its extreme distress.

> Let that obedience be ours which, while it disposes us to listen to our elders and superiors, tests all obedience by the Word of God; in a word, let our church be one whose supreme concern it is humbly and religiously to venerate the Word of God, and submit in obedience to it.

This clear and simple phrase expresses the essential radicalism not only of Calvin but of all subsequent Reformed understanding of authority. Pastors, Calvin states, are not to rule the church "with a wanton and lawless authority." Yet the Church of Rome told its faithful to shut their eyes and submit to their teachers. "Let your Pontiff, then, boast as he may of the succession of Peter . . . so long as he himself maintains his fidelity to Christ, and deviates not from the purity of the gospel."

The Authority of the Word of God in Calvin and the Reformed Churches

The Reformation doctrine of the Word of God is from first to last an attestation of his sovereign will and free grace. As Calvin characteristically expressed it, the Word of God rules within his own church. The church was brought into being through the Word of God; it continues in being and is preserved by the same Word. In the discussion of the church in the *Institutes* Calvin cited John 18:37—"Everyone who is of the truth hears my voice"—to confirm his argument that the church has not produced the Word and can never presume to be superior to it.[2] Christ "reigns by his Word alone," and therefore the true church is always *docilis*, teachable by the Word of God.

To the question of how God's Word is related to scripture, Calvin said that the Word "is comprised" for us in the holy scriptures.[3] The church is founded on the doctrine of the apostles and prophets.[4] On this basis Calvin repudiated the argument of the Romanists that the church had authority over scripture: "These people speak as if they imagined that the mother owed her birth to the daughter."[5] All the Reformers sought to restore the place of scripture in the church. The church must yield obedience to the Bible as the Word of God.

This explains the negative attitude which the Reformed churches have historically taken toward "tradition," if that is

understood to mean a source of revelation or an authority for
the church distinct from scripture. The first decree of the
fourth session of the Council of Trent (April 8, 1546) referred
to "the written books" and "unwritten traditions" pertaining
to faith and manners which were preserved by uninterrupted
succession in the Catholic Church. The former included the so-
called apocryphal writings. The decree anathematized "who-
soever shall not receive these entire books, with all their parts,
as they are accustomed to be read in the Catholic Church, and
are contained in the old Vulgate Latin edition." The second
decree of the session laid it down that none should dare to interpret scripture "contrary to that sense which holy mother
Church, to whom it belongs to judge of the true sense and interpretation of the holy scriptures, has held and holds, or even
contrary to the unanimous consent of the Fathers." The "unwritten traditions" were "received from the lips of Christ himself by the apostles, or as it were handed down by the apostles
themselves, under the inspiration of the Holy Spirit."

In Calvin's *Antidote* to the decree we see the clearest expression of his principle of scriptural authority. As he saw
things, there were four points in dispute. 1. The Romanists ordained that in doctrine we are to stand not on scripture alone,
but on tradition. 2. They insisted on placing the Apocrypha on
the same rank as the undoubted canonical writings. 3. They
repudiated all versions save the Vulgate. 4. Lastly, they
claimed the right of interpreting scripture where the meaning is
doubtful.

Calvin granted that the apostles had handed down to pos-
terity some customs which had not been committed to writing.
But this had nothing to do with the doctrine of faith, only with
external rites. With regard to the Apocrypha, the consent of
the primitive church (*ecclesiae veteris consensus*) was to be de-
terminative. Jerome himself, for instance, regarded books like
Ecclesiasticus and the Maccabees not as canonical but as ecclesiastical books. The apocryphal writings should be consigned to
a lower place. In regard to the condemnation of all versions ex-

cept the Vulgate, it must be admitted, Calvin argued, that this version teemed with innumerable errors. "Nothing is better than to consult the original, in order to obtain the true and genuine meaning." (With this phrase Calvin unalterably set the course of almost all subsequent Reformed biblical criticism and exegesis.) Lastly, in the matter of interpreting scripture where the meaning is obscure—of course, scripture is to be interpreted by the church, Calvin responded, since it is unbecoming to wrest it to anyone's private view. But scripture is to be interpreted in the light of its own uniform testimony.[6] As a notable Reformed confession later expressed it, "The infallible rule of interpretation of scripture is scripture itself, and therefore, when there is a question about the true and full sense of scripture (which is not manifold, but one), it must be searched and known by other places that speak more clearly."[7]

The general principle of scriptural authority has continued within all Reformed churches until the present time. In ordination formulae of an earlier period scripture was typically described in such terms as "the only infallible rule of faith and life" or "the supreme rule of faith and life." More recently the emphasis has shifted, and we find in contemporary formulae of subscription language such as "the normative witness to Jesus Christ in the Church catholic" or "the unique and authoritative witness to Jesus Christ in the church universal, and therefore the authoritative standard by which your faith and life are to be tested."[8]

Within the Reformed churches the authority of scripture has thus been central. Positively, this has meant that these churches have proposed a Christological corrective against any tendency to divinize human authority or to assimilate the Holy Spirit to (for example) the "spirit of Catholicism," or to "follow our own pleasure," as Calvin put it. Not even Martin Luther spoke with stronger conviction about the authority of God's Word for believer and for church. God's Word is given to us in holy scripture, and we are to embrace it there, and subject our minds and wills in obedience to it.

By this scriptural principle the Reformed churches sought not only to define doctrine but to regulate also worship and pastoral discipline. Worship among the Romanists was regarded by Calvin as "nothing but mere corruption," utterly at variance with the Word of God. That Word is the true test by which we must discriminate between what is true in worship and what is false: "The true and sincere worship which God alone approves, and in which he delights, is . . . taught by the Holy Spirit throughout the scriptures."[9] "Popish ceremonies," especially, of course, the Mass with its (to Calvin) objectionable and Pelagian ideas concerning sacrifice, had been introduced into the worship of God without authority from his Word.

The necessity of a scriptural "warrant" for all that is done in worship gave the Reformed or Calvinistic service what has been called its "reverential awe before the sovereign will of grace." Evelyn Underhill wrote:

> Calvin desired a completely spiritual cultus ascending towards a completely spiritual Reality, and rejecting all the humble ritual methods and all the sensible signs by which men are led to express their adoration of the Unseen. . . . Unlike Luther, Calvin was really hostile to the mediaeval embodiments of worship. . . . Hence he cast away without discrimination the whole of the traditional apparatus of Catholicism: its episcopal order, its liturgy, symbols, cultus. No organ or choir was permitted in his churches: no color, no ornament but a table of the Ten Commandments on the wall. No ceremonial acts or gestures were permitted. No hymns were sung but those derived from a Biblical source. The bleak stripped interior of the real Calvinist church is itself sacramental: a witness to the inadequacy of the human over against the Divine.[10]

On the same scriptural grounds Calvin denied the character of a sacrament to any of the seven sacraments of tradition except baptism and the Lord's Supper. His definition of sacrament is that it is "an aid to our faith related to the preaching of the gospel . . . a testimony of divine grace toward us, confirmed by an outward sign, with mutual attestation of our piety toward him."[11] In Reformed theology sacraments are always to be understood as sacraments of the gospel. Calvin was aware that his opponents spoke of a sacrament as consisting of the word and the outward sign. But he argued against them that they had quite misunderstood Augustine at that point. "Let the word be added to the element," the bishop of Hippo had written, "and it will become a sacrament." That word, Calvin said, is the word of the gospel, the word of faith which we proclaim. It is not one whispered without meaning, like a magic incantation to consecrate the element. When Calvin spoke of "word and sign," he did not mean what scholastic theology meant by "form (words) and matter (*res*)." The word, rather, is the promise of the gospel, not a formula of consecration, and the sign is the covenantal sign of baptism or the Supper, joined to preaching with the purpose of confirming and sealing the promise.

Development in Reformed Understandings of Scripture Authority

The church is to be obedient to the Word of God. It has no authority over scripture. The Reformed or Presbyterian churches, however, have not in general regarded scripture as an inerrant oracle-book. If the Bible is the church's book, i.e., the ground of authority for the Christian people, this means that it is the place where we hear the witness of God's revelation to prophets and apostles. Its authority is authenticated by the Holy Spirit. When we hear its witness in faith, it becomes God's very Word to us through the Holy Spirit. "Scripture is indeed self-authenticated," Calvin said. "Hence it is not right to subject it to proof and reasoning. And the certainty it de-

serves with us, it attains by the testimony of the Spirit."[12]
Though Calvin is often credited with the doctrine of the inner
or secret testimony of the Holy Spirit, the doctrine was found
widely in earlier theology. Calvin simply meant that the Bible
is authoritative because it is authenticated by the Spirit. The
Spirit is bound to scripture as the means of its disclosure. Calvin noted that the apostle called preaching "the ministration of
the Spirit," meaning that only when proper reverence and dignity are given to the Word does the Holy Spirit show forth its
power.[13] God bears his own witness to himself, in his Word and
in our hearts. In an eloquent passage Calvin explained the relation between the witness of the Spirit and holy scripture:

> For by a kind of mutual bond the Lord has joined together
> the certainty of his Word and of his Spirit, so that the per-
> fect religion of the Word may abide in our minds when the
> Spirit, who causes us to contemplate God's face, shines;
> and that we in turn may embrace the Spirit with no fear of
> being deceived when we recognize him in his own image,
> namely, in the Word.[14]

In the light of such passages we can discuss what a phrase
such as "development of doctrine" can mean for the Reformed
churches. By the development of doctrine we mean a process
by which the Catholic Church magisterially pronounces such
and such teaching to be a truth contained in the original deposit of revelation, that is, a dogma. The process presupposes a
movement from the original apostolic teaching to the formal
propagation of a dogma. There is an interesting correspondence between the concepts of authority which we find in
sixteenth-century Protestant understandings of biblical authority and certain developments in science of the same period. Medieval science accepted that there were conventional "authorities" (especially the works of Aristotle) which explained the
known universe. Scientific study consisted in proving the authorities right. But as discrepancies arose, the authorities had to

be modified. In the sixteenth and seventeenth centuries, however, mathematicians and philosophers began to see that their task was not to compare and modify authorities, but to relate all authorities to the primary subject matter.

A similar revolution in scientific approach is to be found in Calvin's own principle of biblical interpretation. If "tradition" meant the imposition upon the church of a conventional body of dogmas, and if this tradition was modified little by little from one period to another, then the church's teachers might think that they were truly interpreting the scriptural revelation.

It would have been inconceivable to Calvin to speak of developing or correcting the apostolic teaching. That there will and can be a deepening of understanding, that the Holy Spirit will lead the church into fullness of truth, is, to Reformed churches, not only a thing to be desired but to be prayed for. But the church, being neither infallible nor wholly free from error, can also misunderstand its faith. In doubt, we must constantly refer to the primary authority, scripture. The framers of the Scots Confession (1560) gave it as their opinion that ecumenical councils have erred, "and that in matters of great weight and importance."[15] In each age, therefore, the church must seek to correct its understanding out of the scriptures. And since the church's own interpretations, historically conditioned, can come to occupy the place of scripture teaching, even to contradict it, we must constantly strive to exalt the authority behind all authorities. "We ought not so much to ask what men have said or done before us, as what the Holy Spirit uniformly speaks within the body of the scriptures and what Christ Jesus himself did and commanded."[16]

For Calvin and other reformers of the sixteenth century two unarguable statements were to be made concerning the authority of scripture: first, that scripture communicates the Word of God; and second, that its teaching is clear and unambiguous. He meant that it was clear in the ordinary sense, and that therefore any Christian could understand it; but also that it had the power of bringing its own enlightenment with it, the enlightenment that convinces us of its truth when the Spirit applies the message of scripture to the hearts of those who read it. With these two simple statements the teachers of the Reformed churches lived more or less comfortably at least until the nineteenth century. The age which was ushered in by the French Revolution and came to a climax in the Russian Revolution and the rise of the United States shook all institutions to their foundations and called into question many traditions. Political revolutions accelerated the movement toward secularism. Physics and chemistry were reorganized. Newtonian views of space were revised. The release of pent-up intellectual energies in such areas of study as archaeology, biology and literary criticism threw increasing doubt on the book which still most Christians accepted as authoritative in matters of belief and conduct. Therefore, within the period of the last century or more there can be discerned several ways of responding to the crisis created by this upsurge of scientific and technological thought.

The fundamentalist response was to preserve inviolable Calvin's view of scripture as the authoritative revelation of the will and purpose of God. Though this conservative movement took and still takes many expressions, it was initially a mode of responding to the intellectual crisis of evolution, biblical criticism, and modernism. Fundamentalism sought to protect the essential elements of the Christian faith by emphasizing that the written scriptures are finally authoritative for faith and life. Defenders of this viewpoint commonly say that the scriptures are inspired: the words themselves have been set down by the Holy Spirit, so that we have the pure Word of God free from all human admixture. One of the acknowledged giants in the history of Reformed theology, B. B. Warfield of Princeton, developed his doctrine of biblical inerrancy by arguing that the Holy Spirit not only caused the Word of God to be written down, but providentially ordered that the personality of each writer "has itself been formed by God into precisely the personality it is, for the express purpose of communicating to the Word given through it just the colors which it gives it."[17]

The liberal response was quite different. Many Reformed scholars in the nineteenth and twentieth centuries sought to bring the traditional orthodoxy of Calvin into closer alignment with modern philosophy, science and historical criticism. Continuing to affirm that the Bible, rightly understood, remains authoritative for faith and life, advocates of this point of view rejected the intellectualism of Reformed orthodoxy, and adopted more or less wholeheartedly a critical view of the Bible. The contribution of liberal scholars to the understanding of the Bible has been large, notably in biblical criticism, scripture commentaries, comparative religion, form criticism and the history of traditions. The liberal approach to biblical authority is of particular interest to us in regard to the ideas of progressive revelation and of inspiration. If it is true that the Bible discloses to us not propositions about God but God himself, then we are to recognize that the scriptures indicate how unworthy conceptions of God were gradually stripped away, until finally his purest revelation of himself is given in Jesus Christ. This view of the Bible is common today in many Reformed churches, and its strength (and also weakness) is that it attempts to reconcile an authoritative view of the Bible with the human and historical side of its composition. With regard to the inspiration of the Bible, John Baillie is perhaps typical. He readily regarded parts of the Bible as inspired, for instance, 1 Corinthians 13, but clearly the Bible as a whole was not.[18]

In marked contrast with other contemporary approaches to the authority of the Bible Karl Barth took up the study of scripture with a new seriousness. It is well known that according to Barth the Word of God assumes three forms: as the Word of God preached, as the written Word of God, and as the revealed Word of God. Barth's methodology in *Church Dogmatics* is to be clearly distinguished from the classical Calvinism of, for instance, the Westminster Confession (1647). The Confession began with a chapter on scripture, as fine a statement within its limits as can be found. Yet it repeated the tendency of Protestant orthodoxy to identify revelation with the scriptures: "It pleased the Lord, at sundry times, and in divers manners, to reveal himself, and to declare his will unto his church; and afterwards, for the better preserving and propagating of the truth . . . to commit the same wholly unto writing."[19] Barth denied that the Word of God proclaimed or written had an inherent divine power, whatever its effect on the hearer or reader might be. The Bible *becomes* the Word of God whenever God makes it the vehicle of his speaking to us. Its authority is not to be based on any theory of inspiration but upon God's freedom in making the proclamation of the scripture his own Word. In this context, to use an older Reformed proposition, "the preaching of the Word of God *is* the Word of God." The Bible is not itself the revelation; it contains no truths revealed by God.

> The statement that the Bible is God's Word cannot mean that the Bible, among other attributes, also has the attribute of being God's Word. This would be to encroach on the Word of God which is God himself. . . . The fact that the Bible witnesses to God's revelation does not mean that God's revelation lies before us in some sort of divine revealedness. The Bible is no book of oracles; it is no organ of direct communication.[20]

The Bible is attestation and witness to revelation. Only the free decision of God produces the event in which the Bible and revelation become one: to speak of the Word of God is to speak of the work of God. God makes the record of what was revealed in the past the occasion of present revelation.[21]

On what grounds, then, according to Barth, can we hold the Bible to be authoritative? Barth discusses the question at length in *Church Dogmatics*, Volume I, part 2, chapters 3 and 4. To speak of authority in the church, he says, is to speak of scripture. Authority presupposes obedience. And scripture bears witness to the apostles and prophets who are obedient servants. They do not constitute authority in themselves. But we receive their witness in scripture to the authority to which they render obedience: "This authentic reconstruction of the revelation and this authentic example of obedience rendered to it is the content of the witness of the prophets and apostles in holy scripture."[22] The error of the Roman Catholic Church is that it claims authority for itself; its definitions of dogma are "of themselves irreformable." But there is another error, that of the Enthusiasts who bypass scripture. Against both stands the authority of scripture, by which alone the church is called to live its life.

Barth's view of the authority of scripture has been widely influential in contemporary Protestantism. His insistence on the Bible as witness and his concept of revelation as event or encounter destroyed any bibliolatry and sanctioned the critical textual study of modern biblical scholarship. To designate the Bible as witness to God's revelation was of value, because it precluded the easy and uncritical identity of the Bible and the Word of God. Nevertheless, Barth himself has been criticized, for instance, by James Barr, who argued (by means of Barth's own Christological analogy) that scripture is not only analogous to Christ the Word who comes from God, but to Jesus of Nazareth who speaks a word of obedience to God from within mankind. "The Christological analogy is not properly used if we relate the Bible only to the entry of God into the world in the incarnation; we have to relate it also to Christ's priestly mission, and to the ascension."[23]

In summary, the following would generally be accepted by Reformed theologians and teachers who have been influenced by Barth, and would regard themselves as neither Fundamentalist nor Liberals:

First, the Bible is a witness to revelation, and is not itself the Word of God. The witness is always different from that to which it witnesses. We therefore have to hear what the Bible as a human word has to say.

Second, inspiration means the act of revelation, in which the prophets and apostles in all their humanness became the witnesses they were, and in which alone they in all their humanness can become for us the witnesses they are.

Third, as the authority of scripture does not lie in its indefectibility or infallibility, so the assailability of the human word in the Bible is no ground for rejecting its authority. The authority of scripture lies beyond the words of the page of scripture in the free and sovereign act of God.

The Right To Modify Forms of Belief

In chapter III, "Of God's Eternal Decrees," the Westminster Confession of Faith gave expression to the *decretum horribile* which was to dominate in much seventeenth- and eighteenth-century Calvinism: "By the decree of God, for the manifestation of his glory, some men and angels are predestined unto everlasting life, and others foreordained to everlasting death."

By any definition the doctrine of double predestination has a prominent position in the Confession. It comes after the chapters on scripture and God the Holy Trinity and before the chapters on creation and Christ. Is such a doctrine one on which there can possibly be "liberty of opinion"? For centuries it was undoubtedly regarded within the Reformed churches as a fundamental doctrine, and if modern Calvinism has moved almost wholly away from such expressions, it does so clearly against its own tradition. So we must inquire into the grounds on which such a radical separation from traditional understandings took place.

In the nineteenth century a saintly and scholarly parish minister called John McLeod Campbell, of Row, Scotland, entered upon his ministry in loyalty to Westminster orthodoxy concerning the decrees. But in the course of dealing with his parishioners, he found them struggling with doubts and uncertainty about their own salvation, and by the end of his ministry was proclaiming universal atonement through Christ: "That cannot be the true conception of the atonement which implies that Christ died . . . for the elect only."[24] In saying this, Campbell was clearly going against the prevailing stream of Reformed thought on the question. The "bearing and general impression of the scriptures," Campbell wrote, makes it plain that any doctrine of limited atonement "destroys the claim of the work of Christ to be what fully reveals and illustrates the great foundation of all religion, that God is love."[25] Campbell's contribution to Reformed understandings of scripture in and beyond his day was to revert to the older principle of interpretation: we must listen to what the Holy Spirit speaks within scripture and to what Jesus Christ himself did and commanded. The church can be free to modify the forms of orthodox belief and allow a reasonable liberty of opinion by holding "the bearing and general impression of the scriptures" against those doctrines in the confession that do not enter into the substance of the Reformed faith.

The idea of scripture as its own best interpreter was not a circular argument for the theologians of the Reformed churches, though no doubt it helped to produce the sterile biblicism which isolated the study of the Bible from life in the world.[26] Rather, it made possible a double differentiation. On the one hand it made possible a distinction between the substance of a doctrine and the way in which it is presented. Through literary and historical criticism, notably in the nineteenth and twentieth centuries, Protestant scholars have inquired into the historical setting of the confessions and scriptural exegesis of their own churches. Thereby they learned to distinguish between what is central in Christian doctrine and the language and forms of thought in which the teaching is expressed. But they also sought to draw another distinction between "fundamental doctrines" and those where differences of opinion are allowable. As early as 1729 American Presbyterians adopted an overture in which the Westminster stan-

dards were described as being "in all the essential and necessary articles good forms of sound words and systems of
Christian doctrine." But these essential articles were distinguished from "extra-essential and not necessary points of doctrine."[27] Until fairly recently the United Presbyterian Church
in the U.S.A. required its candidates for ordination to sub-
scribe to a declaration that they regarded the Westminster
Confession of Faith "as containing the system of doctrine
taught in the Holy Scriptures." This was often interpreted to
mean that acceptance of a system was not the same thing as
accepting individually every doctrine in the Confession. A similar distinction is drawn in the ordination formula of the Church
of Scotland:

> The Church of Scotland holds as its subordinate standard
> the Westminster Confession of Faith, recognizing liberty
> of opinion on such points of doctrine as do not enter into
> the substance of the Faith, and claiming the right, in de-
> pendence on the promised guidance of the Holy Spirit, to
> formulate, interpret, or modify its subordinate standards:
> always in agreement with the Word of God and the fun-
> damental doctrines of the Christian Faith contained in the
> said Confession—of which agreement the Church itself
> shall be sole judge.[28]

The phrase "system of doctrine" is ambiguous, perhaps
deliberately so, and the distinction in the Scottish ordinal between "fundamental doctrines" and "such points of doctrine as
do not enter into the substance of the Faith" may be merely a
restatement of the problem rather than a solution to it. Both of
the formulas, however, attempted to distinguish between what
is basic or fundamental in Christian doctrine and what is not.
To the extent that they freed the Reformed churches, except
for the more conservative branches, from the rigidity of Calvinistic orthodoxy, they have been helpful. Most Presbyterians
today would accept that some teachings are "central," and

others not so important; few would regard "double predestination" as central, at least in its seventeenth-century garb. But the distinction may also be deceptive and misleading. If what generations of Presbyterians regarded as central and fundamental can be treated as "not entering into the substance of the faith," could the same treatment be given to, say, the doctrine of the Trinity? Most Presbyterians would say no, and continue to hold belief in God as triune; and they would do so on some such grounds as "the bearing and general impression of the scriptures" or a similar statement. Here, again, the principle of scripture as its own best interpreter applies. It should be noted that Karl Barth himself parted company with Calvin on the doctrine of election precisely on the assertion that the subject of the decision in election is the triune God, i.e., the *Word* who was incarnate for our salvation no less than the Father and the Spirit. Barth sought to give Christ a more central place in the doctrine of election, which means that he sought to use Calvin's own method of biblical interpretation.

Councils and the Word of God

In Calvin's view the Word of God provides us with the standard by which all ecclesiastical government or "regiment" is to be tested. He was a good historian, familiar with the early church, and he respected both the spirit and the letter of the ancient councils. In fact, with regard to the election and appointment of those who were to rule in the church, he sought to apply the conciliar decrees as far as possible. His quarrel with the bishops of his day was that their election was uncanonical, lacking as it did the order which the apostles observed in ordaining ministers, that which the primitive church afterward followed, and finally that which the ancient canons require to be observed.[29] The government and common order of the church are preserved, Calvin insisted, by scripture, primitive precedent and usage, and the canons of the first ecumenical councils.

In the preface to the *Antidote* Calvin quoted Augustine with approval for bestowing honor on councils, insofar as they were founded on the authority of scripture. But councils are not inerrant.[30] Most later Reformed confessions reiterated this point with emphasis. The Scots Confession, for example, stated: "We do not receive uncritically whatever has been declared to men under the name of the general councils, for it is plain that, being human, some of them have manifestly erred, and that in matters of great weight and importance. So far then as the council confirms its decrees by the plain Word of God, so far do we reverence and embrace them."[31] Calvin's opposition to the Council of Trent was that it would fail to establish the truth of the case from scripture, since he feared that the council would be "nothing else than a hired crew" of the pope's own followers. Nothing would be determined at Trent save at the nod of the pope. Calvin asked if anyone could be so stupid as to seek any alleviation of the present evils of the church from a council. The Romanists used such bombastic language as "sacrosanct," "ecumenical," "universal synod," and "lawfully met in the Holy Spirit," but there were, perhaps, forty bishops present at the first session—"and this," Calvin expostulated, "is what they call a universal council!"

Shortly after the Reformation was introduced into Scotland the General Assembly ordered a confession, usually known as the Second Helvetic, to be printed, following its acceptance by the Reformed churches in Geneva, Savoy, Poland, and Hungary, though not by the Church of England, "becaus of the manie corruptions mainteaned by them, which are condemned in it."[32] Article I of the Helvetic Confession affirmed belief in the scriptures as the Word of God, and Article II declared that the Fathers, councils and traditions of the church are of high, but secondary, authority. Article XI explicitly listed the first four ecumenical councils:

We sincerely believe and freely profess whatsoever things are defined out of the holy scriptures in the Creeds, and in the decrees of those first four and most excellent Councils

—held at Nicaea, Constantinople, Ephesus, and Chalcedon—together with blessed Athanasius' Creed, and all
Creeds like to these. . . . Thus we retain the Christian
sound and Catholic Faith, whole and inviolable, knowing
that nothing is contained in the aforesaid Creeds which is
not agreeable to the Word of God.

Since the signatories of the Helvetic Confession included
John Knox and others who had helped to frame the earlier
Scots Confession (1560), the Scottish Reformers clearly intended to assert the right of the Reformed churches to the name of
Catholic and their possession of Catholic doctrine. The Scots
Confession had earlier explicitly condemned "the damnable
and pestilent heresies" of Arius, Marcion, Eutyches, Nestorius,
and others,[33] and the Westminster Confession used the explicit
language of Chalcedon in its declaration concerning Christ.
Both the ecumenical councils and the Catholic creeds constitut-
ed for the Reformed churches an authoritative witness to the
apostolic gospel.[34]

Church Government and the Word of God

In Geneva the pastors and elders formed the Consistory,
an ecclesiastical tribunal responsible for disciplinary oversight.
Its chief strength lay in its power of excommunication. The
ministers were further required to attend quarterly meetings—
the "Vénérable Compagnie"—for mutual criticism and admo-
nition. In these two bodies the earliest expressions of Presbyterian government are to be found. In its developed form Presbyterian government first appeared in the so-called second
Book of Discipline (adopted by the Church of Scotland in
1581). This famous document was the work of Andrew Melville, who earlier in his life had learned to hate despotism and to
love liberty in republican Geneva. "Hot and eager upon any
thing he went about," as an early historian described him, Mel-

ville was listened to with respect when he pronounced his views
on bishops. The Assembly of the Reformed church in 1575 had
inquired "whether bishops as they were then in Scotland had
their function warranted by the Word of God." Melville's own
view was that Christ allowed no superiority among his ministers, and the Assembly approved the statement "that they
judged the name of a bishop to be common to all ministers that
had the charge of a particular flock."[35] For the next few years
the Assembly was "busied with the matter of policy," i.e.,
church government, and in April 1581 resolved that "the Book
of Policy," more commonly known as the Book of Discipline,
should be registered in the acts of the Kirk *ad perpetuam rei
memoriam*. Since the document expounds the scheme of
church government by which most Presbyterian churches were
subsequently regulated, it is necessary to sketch it briefly, especially in the matter of authority.

The church, it was stated, "hath a certain power granted
by God, according to which it useth a proper jurisdiction and
government." This power ecclesiastical is granted by God, has
its ground in the Word of God, and is to be administered by
those to whom the spiritual government of the church is committed. This power differs from what is called civil power. Both
flow from God, but a broad distinction between the power of
the sword and the power of the keys is to be maintained. The
second chapter dealt with the office-bearers of the church.
"There are four ordinary offices or functions in the Church of
God; the pastor, minister, or bishop, the doctor, the presbyter
or elder, and the deacon." These offices were to continue permanently in the church. In the fourth chapter the duties of
"pastors, bishops, or ministers" were defined. Pastors are appointed to particular congregations, which they are to rule by
the Word of God. To them it belongs to preach, administer the
sacraments, solemnize marriage, pray for the people, watch
over the manners of the flock, and pronounce the sentence of
binding and loosing, according to the power of the keys granted to the church. The seventh chapter is an important one and

referred to the assemblies of the church. "Assemblies are of four sorts; for either they are of a particular congregation, or of a province, or of a whole nation, or of all and divers Christian nations." The first sort of assembly is that within particular congregations. Provincial assemblies are "lawful conventions of the pastors, doctors, and other elders of any province gathered for the common affairs of the churches thereof." The national assembly, also called General Assembly, "is a lawful convention of the whole church of the realm or nation where it is gathered, for the common affairs of the church." Finally, there is besides these "another more general assembly, which is of all nations, and of all estates of persons within the church, representing the universal Church of Christ, which may be properly called the general assembly, or general council of the whole Church of God."[36]

In Melville's policy we see both the strengths and the weaknesses of the post-Reformation church: its strengths in the comity rather than balance it achieved between the two powers, ecclesiastical and civil—what Melville called "the two kingdoms"—and its insistence on the spiritual freedom of the church established by law; and its weaknesses in its combination of theocratic pretensions and sectarian mentality. As Presbyterian polity spread into other parts of the world, it took with it in its development the characteristic shape given to it by Melville. Nowadays its system of graded courts (for instance, in the United States) is usually that of the church session or classis (in the local congregation), the presbytery (consisting of all the ministers and one elder from each of the churches within a particular district), the synod (consisting of a number of presbyteries in a particular region or province), and the General Assembly (representing in equal numbers the ministers and elders of each presbytery). While some of its staunch defenders have held to Presbyterianism as *iure divino*, the only polity allowable by scripture, most have regarded it rather as "agreeable to the Word of God." Had the more rigorist view prevailed, Presbyterians would not have been able to agree so

easily to such ecumenical arrangements as the Consultation of
Church Union has proposed, or to participate in united
churches, as in South or North India.

Reformed Rejection of Papal Claims

The rejection of papal claims of primacy by the Reformed
churches has been absolute from the beginning. The rejection
was based on two beliefs about the Word of God and its authority. First, it was held, there is no scriptural warrant for the
papacy. "Scripture," Calvin wrote, "often mentions Christ the
universal Head, but nowhere mentions the pope."[37] Paul spoke
of one Lord, one faith, one baptism, not of one pope. He
defended his apostleship to the Gentiles as "equal to that which
Peter received toward the Jews." From this we may infer that
the apostleship of Peter does not properly extend to us.

Second, papal claims of a primacy of honor or of jurisdiction are belied by the failure of the pope to exercise a true episcopal ministry. In one of his writings Calvin quotes Augustine
with approval: "Bishopric is the name of an office, and not a
mere title of honor." The ancient synods defined the bishop's
office as "feeding the people by preaching the Word, in administering the sacraments, in curbing clergy and people by
holy discipline, and, in order not to be distracted from these
duties, in withdrawing from all the ordinary cares of the present life."[38] Which of these, Calvin complained, do the pope and
his cardinals pretend to perform?

Reformed churches since the sixteenth century have generally followed Calvin in rejecting any papal claims of primacy
not only on the basis of scripture but by the *prima facie* evidence of corruption and venality in both the curia and the
papal office itself. Calvin, it must be conceded, set the example
for papal critics and detractors who followed him. Leo X was
"cruel," Clement VII "bloodstained," and Paul III "trucu-
lent." The Roman see was "possessed by impious superstitions,

open idolatry, perverse doctrines," while the great truths in which the Christian religion consists have been suppressed.[39]

The sixteenth century was a notoriously intolerant age, and Calvin's language is to be judged in this light. Nevertheless, his criticism had substance. More to the point, it had long precedent. A century and a half earlier Marsilius of Padua in his *Defensor Pacis* (1324) had expressed a deep dissatisfaction with conditions in the church. The papacy itself, Marsilius had written, was an intolerable usurpation, incompatible with scripture, and dangerous for the peace of Europe. William of Occam's attack in the *Dialogue* (1343) by citing authorities for and against the papacy had made it uncertain whether the papacy had the authority that it claimed. The Roman Catholic historian, Joseph Lortz, spoke of the Reformation as an "historical necessity." If it was, Calvin is to be seen at the end of a line of critics of abuses that can be traced back to the Avignon papacy.

Calvin had no intention of annihilating the authority of the church or of the leaders and pastors to whom the superintendence of its government had been given. Bishops and pastors, he said, should be reverently listened to, on the grounds of decency and order. Laws and statutes were to be obeyed, insofar as they did not bind consciences or foster superstition. But a distinction was to be drawn between true and false pastors, and papal claims to authority in the church were to be denied because the bishop of Rome was not a true pastor. Commenting on the words "in God's sanctuary" in 2 Thessalonians 2:4 (the antichrist "enthrones himself in God's sanctuary and claims that he is God"), Calvin wrote: "This one word fully refutes the error or rather stupidity of those who hold the pope to be the vicar of Christ." That is, the primacy which the pope attributes to himself is a usurpation.[40] Calvin's attack was directed chiefly against the attitude which the popes took toward the gospel. The error of the papacy was that it had bound the honor of primacy to a *place*. Merely to occupy the see which was once the first see of all does not make its incumbent

Christ's vicar or Peter's successor. Indeed, the pope had become "Christ's most hateful enemy."[41] As for the papal hierarchy, Calvin was as trenchant in his criticism as he was of the
papacy. The church should be governed by the pastors to
whom has been committed the office of preaching and administering the sacraments. But the popish hierarchy has been established "for the very purpose of making God himself to be
despised, and of exposing the Christian religion to mockery
and scorn."[42]

There can be little question that Calvin's severe and con-
demnatory criticism of papal primacy and of the Roman Catholic concept of authority both sanctioned and sharpened all
later religious controversies in which Catholics and Protestants
have confronted one another. At a painfully low level of human
relationships the conflict in Northern Ireland has brought to
the surface a tainted and deep-seated inheritance of hostility
toward ideas of papal theocracy and clerical tyranny. Even at
a higher level, Protestant sects which include the designation
"Reformed" or "Bible" in their official names have tended to
perpetuate a suspicion of "Catholicism."

The ecclesiology of a liberal Protestant like Auguste Sabatier, a professor of Reformed dogmatics at Strassburg from
1867 to 1873, could be regarded as a widely-held statement of
principle among many Reformed churches. Protestantism, he
wrote, "is not a dogma set up in the face of another dogma, a
Church in competition with a rival Church, a purified Catholicism opposed to a traditional Catholicism. It is more and better than a doctrine, it is a method; more and better than a better Church, it is a new form of piety; it is a different spirit,
creating a new world and inaugurating for religious souls a new
regime."[43] Even a modern Presbyterian scholar, by no means
to be regarded as anti-ecumenical, can write:

Certain aspects of the Roman doctrine of the Church and
her ordering and government are seen as inconsistent with
a true understanding of the Church. The Roman attempt

to identify the Church by its hierarchy of government, rather than by the reformed marks of the true Church, is held to be essentially false. The Bishop of Rome's office as Pope or Supreme Pontiff, further, obscures the sole Kingship and Headship of Jesus Christ in his Church and is accordingly unbiblical and doctrinally misleading.[44]

Over the centuries the Reformed rejection of papal primacy and its hierarchy of government has been grounded on a scriptural basis, defended theologically, preached and proclaimed, taught in its seminaries and schools. Its confessions of faith and even its prayers have been colored by this great denial. "Seeing we live now in these most perilous times," John Knox prayed in his Liturgy (1560), "defend us against the violence of all our enemies, but chiefly against the wicked rage and furious uproars of that Romish idol, enemy to thy Christ." The hatred—it is not too strong a word—which has underlain the attitude taken toward the Roman Catholic Church by theologians, pastors, and people of the churches that have followed Calvin has never been universal, but it has often fed upon itself and its poison will only slowly be drawn.

The Reformed Churches and the Papacy

The question can be asked: Are there any conditions under which the Reformed churches could accept the Roman Catholic concept of papal primacy? Reformed scholars would tend to answer: What concept? Concepts of papal primacy have altered markedly in the history of the church. In the age of the councils, for example, it became evident to a number of theologians that the Catholic Church could be given a single pope again only by denying, in effect, that the papacy was the best way by which the church can be governed. Hence the conciliar theorists went back to an older concept, namely that the fullness of the church consists in the corporate body of all the faithful. John Gerson argued in his *De potestate ecclesiastica*

that the *plenitudo potestatis* of the church resided in its whole
body, as represented by a general council. In the modern
period, a noted Protestant theologian commented that the collegial notion of the hierarchy in the *Dogmatic Constitution on
the Church* of Vatican Council II "opens a new era in Roman
Catholic conceptions of Church order." The understanding, he
went on, "is a striking advance beyond the sterile extremes of
traditional 'ultramontanism,' on the one hand, and traditional
'conciliarism' on the other."[45]

So the first approach by Reformed scholars to the controversial question of papal primacy would be one of inquiry—
biblical, doctrinal and historical. Since 1965 the Roman Catho-
lic/Reformed and Presbyterian Consultation in the United
States has studied various aspects of the problem. In 1971 the
following agreements were clarified: First, in all that we say
about church and ministry we start with Christ himself and his
own ministry. Second, there is a general ministry or common
priesthood of all who are baptized, and this common priesthood provides the context in which we treat the ordained
priesthood, or the specific ministry of Word and sacraments.
In regard to apostolic succession the consultants stated that
however much they may differ on the methods of maintaining
them, both traditions agree on the necessity of continuity and
succession in the apostolic life, doctrine, and ministry of the
church. Finally, the statement dealt with two critical questions
with which the Reformed churches have difficulty: papal claims
to primacy and universal jurisdiction in church government,
and to infallibility in teaching.

The growing awareness in the Reformed churches of the
need for effective worldwide unifying forms, and in
Roman Catholicism of the collegial context and pastoral
character of the papal role opens the way to new possibilities in the first problem area. On the local level the contemporary church needs a creative fusing of the episcopal
and presbyteral/congregational traditions. So, too, on a

much wider scale the church needs, in a spirit of pastoral service, to blend the unifying drive which a papacy of the future might provide, with the vitalizing growth which can come from the "collegial" or representative spirit inherent in the Reformed tradition. Hence, one of the main questions may prove to be how effectively the conciliar and representative pattern can be fused at the world level with individual personal leadership. There will also need to be careful exploration as to precisely what kinds and what degree of ecclesiastical jurisdiction are appropriate at each level: regional, national and worldwide. Consequently, although our churches are presently divided in habits of thought and practice, as is true of both Roman Catholics and Presbyterian-Reformed Christians among themselves, it is clearly to the advantage, both of the universal church —and also of the world to which it witnesses and ministers —that we learn from each other and act jointly in this regard.

The statement continues by speaking of infallibility:

There may well have been times when papal centralism best responded to the needs of a given historical moment; the right of the Church to respond to these needs cannot be denied. The doctrine of infallibility received its classical form in the last century at a time when papal authority was being vigorously reaffirmed. In other historical periods, however, there have been other ways in which the Petrine function has been exercised. Therefore, when one speaks of infallibility, or any other exercise of papal authority, papal centrism need not be considered the only style of exercising the Petrine function. The model of collegiality, for instance, is one whose implications have not yet been fully explored.[46]

A Constitutional and Evangelical Papacy?

In 1844 Philip Schaff was appointed first professor of
church history at the newly-formed seminary of the German
Reformed Church in Mercersburg, Pennsylvania. In his inaugural address, printed in the following year as *The Principle of
Protestantism*, Schaff described his vision of an evangelical
Catholic Church which united the best features of Protestantism and Catholicism. Schaff was one of the most capable
church historians of his age, and his views have increasingly
influenced the more advanced ecumenical thinking in the Reformed churches since his sentiments burst like a bombshell in
a nation of strongly anti-Catholic sentiment. According to
Schaff, the history of the church is to be understood as an organic development in which each new stage of history grows
out of and fulfills the preceding stage. Protestantism would be
consummated by coming into reconciliation with Catholicism
finally "in a higher position, in which all past errors shall be
left behind whether Protestant or Catholic, and the truth of
both tendencies be actualized, as the power of one and the
same life, in the full revelation of the kingdom of God."[47]
Christianity in origin was Petrine, stressing the law and authority, and ending in the papacy. At the Reformation it became
Pauline, a religion of freedom and enlargement. In the future it
would be Johannine, when the antagonism and antithesis of all
the preceding ages would be reconciled in a higher synthe-
sis.[48]

Seven years after the First Vatican Council Schaff published the first volume of *The Creeds of Christendom*.[49] In his
discussion of the Vatican Council and especially its dogma of
infallibility Schaff sought to test whether the dogma was a
truly Catholic interpretation of scripture and tradition. On
both grounds he found it wanting. But there was a truth within
the "colossal lie of the papacy," namely the primacy assigned
to Peter among the apostles. The error of the papacy was that
it perverted a primacy of honor into a supremacy of jurisdic-

tion and a priority of time into a permanent superiority of rank. Schaff accused Rome of identifying "the true ideal Church of Christ with the empirical Church, and the empirical Church with the Romish Church, and the Romish Church with the papacy, and the papacy with the pope."[50]

In an essay published in the year of his death, 1893, Schaff urged upon the divided churches a reconsideration of the problems that continued to divide them. If any one church is to be the center of unification, he said, that honor would be conceded to either the Greek or the Roman communion. He expressed the hope that Rome might make the concessions necessary so that it could become such a center. Then, hazarding a suggestion to deal with the impasse which the decree of 1870 had created nearly a generation earlier, Schaff asked:

> What if the pope, in the spirit of the first Gregory and under the inspiration of a higher authority, should infallibly declare his own fallibility in all matters lying outside of his own communion? Would this open a way for him to invite Greeks and Protestants to a fraternal pan-Christian council in Jerusalem, where the mother-church of Christendom held the first council of reconciliation and peace?[51]

Schaff did not explain to his hearers what he had in mind. Presumably the proposed council would direct itself to the ecumenical obstacle represented by the infallibility decree.

The Reformed churches have not until recently considered what changes in the Roman Catholic understanding of the papacy would be necessary before any reconciliation might be achieved. Schaff was a notable exception in the nineteenth century. In the twentieth century similar ideas were expressed by William Edwin Orchard, an English Presbyterian who served as minister of the King's Weigh House Church in London from 1914 until the time of his conversion to the Roman Catholic Church in 1932. Orchard preached and wrote widely on ecumenical questions. He shared Schaff's vision that a movement was taking place toward what he called a freer type of Catholicism, uniting the oppositions of the church in a glorious whole.

> It is therefore possible to hold [he wrote in 1926] that one day the form which the Roman Church has preserved will be found capable of a much wider and more generous interpretation; that with that interpretation the. other Churches will be brought into communion with Rome; that with the putting aside of temporal policy, of all attempts to lord it over the brethren, the historic claims of the Petrine see will be accepted by Christendom.[52]

Among those who have given consideration to the possibility of a modified papacy in theological writings or in ecumenical conversations, the following ideas seem to recur.

First, there is no prospect of organic union of the Reformed churches with the Roman Catholic Church as long as an "imperial papacy" exists. The Reformed churches will not lightly seek unity with the Roman Catholic Church, and under no conditions, if they must abandon the liberties and rights of conscience which they achieved through the turmoil of the Reformation.

Second, while the Reformed churches are, of course, deeply concerned in ecumenical conversations about matters of faith and order, and while they concede that some orders are in certain circumstances better than others to serve the purposes of the Holy Spirit, yet they are not willing to concede that any particular order is necessary to all churches in all periods.

Third, and related to this, it is conceivable that a restatement of the doctrine of authority—for which the bilateral consultations may provide a theological context—could stress the function of the papacy primarily in terms of service and only minimally of jurisdiction. The worst argument for the papacy, in the Reformed understanding, was the medieval papacy in its decline; and the best argument would not be a theory of Petrine succession but popes who showed in their own personal lives a love of the gospel and a desire to serve the needs of the world.

Fourth, significant numbers of Protestants today could conceive that the papacy might be reformed in such a way that its true power lay not in any theory of continuity as such but in its pastoral character.

Fifth, the Reformed churches have shown a readiness to leave behind the bitterness of their own polemic against Rome and consider afresh the meaning of the Petrine office. At a theological level a book like *Peter in the New Testament*[53] demonstrates what exegetical and historical research can produce.

Sixth, there is no possibility that the papal office could ever become acceptable to the Reformed churches unless it were clearly and radically freed from its almost exclusively Italian character. If a reformed and constitutionalized papacy is ever to be possible, the office would presumably have to be open to any nationality.

Seventh, the Reformed churches, bound as they are inseparably to the Word of God, will always remember that Peter in the New Testament is both the rock and the stumbling block. "For me," Hendrikus Berkhof wrote in 1969, "the main ecumenical question with regard to the Petrine office is this: Is the officeholder capable of existentially embodying in himself the unique and at the same time exemplary dialectic of this function?" Peter was the rocklike foundation of the church precisely as the one who was saved from sin, as he who is constantly carried by the Lord. What then can the pope do? Berkhof asked. "He must die as pope in order to rise again as Peter. In other words, he must lose his *auctoritas* and *potestas* (authority and power) in order to win them."[54]

Last, and by no means least, the Reformed churches must constantly remember that the call of Christ is a call to *metanoia*. To be true to the Reformation does not mean to echo in our day the legitimate protests of Luther and Calvin and those who came after them. To be truly "reformed" means always to listen afresh to the Word of God as a reality higher than any of our traditions, as that which judges us and our past, and calls us into a new future, a future that is not our making but God's. In the *Plan of Union* (1970), commended to the churches for study by the Consultation on Church Union, the participating churches (including the major Presbyterian and Reformed bodies in the United States) declared: "We envisage a united church, embodying all that is indispensable to each of us, and bearing enough family resemblance to our separate traditions to verify their continuity in it, yet unlike the churches any of us has known in our past separateness."

Eric Mascall concludes one of his books with an imaginative quotation from Vergil's first Eclogue. The dialogue is between Tityrus and Meliboeus:

Tityrus: I soon saw that Rome stands out above all other cities as the cypress soars above the drooping undergrowth.
Meliboeus: And what was the urgent business that took you to Rome?
Tityrus: Liberty.

"Of old," Calvin wrote in the *Institutes*, "Rome was indeed the mother of all churches; but it ceased to be what it once was." May God grant in our age, and if not ours then in our children's, that all the churches may again have recourse to this church (which is possibly the meaning of a controverted phrase in St. Irenaeus) because of its leadership and authority. But it must be a leadership in service and an authority in the gospel, in which alone we enjoy what the apostle, who was martyred there, called "freedom and glory as the children of God."

NOTES

1. Text in John Calvin, *Tracts and Treatises on the Reformation of the Church* (= *TT*), vol. 1, p. 14. Grand Rapids, Michigan: Wm. B. Eerdmans Publishing Company, repr. 1958.

2. John Calvin, *Institutes of the Christian Religion* (= *Inst.*) 4:2:4. The edition used is the Library of Christian Classics, vol. XX, ed. John T. Mc-Neill, tr. by Ford Lewis Battles. Philadelphia: The Westminster Press, 1960.

3. *Catechism of the Church of Geneva*, 1541, in *TT*, vol. 2, p. 82.

4. *The True Method of Giving Peace to Christendom*, in *TT*, vol. 3, p. 267.

5. *Ibid.*

6. *Antidote to the Decree*, in *TT*, vol. 3, p. 74.

7. Westminster Confession of Faith, 1:9.

8. See the revised or proposed subscription questions of both the United Presbyterian Church in the U.S.A. and the Presbyterian Church, U.S.

9. *On the Necessity of Reforming the Church*, in *TT*, vol. 1, p. 127.

10. Evelyn Underhill, *Worship*, p. 287. London: Nisbet & Co. Ltd., repr. 1951.

11. *Inst.* 4:14:1.

12. *Inst.* 1:7:5.

13. *Inst.* 1:9:3.

14. *Ibid.*

15. Scots Confession, art. XX.

16. *Ibid.*, art. XVIII.

17. B.B. Warfield, *The Inspiration and Authority of the Bible*, pp. 155ff. Philadelphia: Presbyterian and Reformed Publishing Company, repr. 1948.

18. John Baillie, *The Idea of Revelation in Recent Thought*, pp. 115-120. New York: Columbia University Press, 1956.

19. Westminster Confession of Faith, 1:1.

20. Karl Barth, *Church Dogmatics* (= CD), vol. I, pt. 2, p. 562. Edinburgh: T & T Clark, 1956.

21. See J. K. S. Reid, *The Authority of Scripture*, p. 200. London: Methuen, 1957.

22. *CD* I, 2, p. 605.

23. James Barr, review of J. K. S. Reid, *The Authority of Scripture*, in *Scottish Journal of Theology*, vol. 11, no. 1 (1958), pp. 86-93.

24. J. McLeod Campbell, *The Nature of the Atonement*, pp. 51, 53. 6th edition. London: 1906.

25. *Ibid.*, p. 56.

26. John H. Leith, *Assembly at Westminster*, pp. 75-84. Richmond, Va., John Knox Press, 1973.

27. *The Presbyterian Digest*, p. 45. Philadelphia, 1886.

28. *Practice and Procedure in the Church of Scotland*, ed. by James T. Cox, p. 534. Edinburgh and London: William Blackwood & Sons, 1948.

29. *The Necessity of Reforming the Church*, in *TT*, vol. 1, pp. 170-176.

30. *Preface to the Antidote*, in *TT*, vol. 3, pp. 33ff.

31. Scots Confession, art. XX:3. Cf. also Westminster, Confession of Faith, 33:3.

32. David Calderwood, *The History of the Church of Scotland*, vol. II, pp. 331ff. Edinburgh, 1843.

33. Scots Confession, art. VI.

34. See H. J. Wotherspoon and J. M. Kirkpatrick, *A Manual of Church Doctrine*, revised and enlarged by T. F. Torrance and Ronald Selby Wright, pp. 59-68. London: Oxford University Press, 1960.

35. John Spottiswoode, *History of the Church of Scotland*, vol. II, p. 201. Edinburgh, 1851.

36. Text in David Calderwood, *The History of the Kirk of Scotland*, vol. III, pp. 529-554. Edinburgh, 1843.

37. *Antidote to Article XXIII of the Articles by the Theological Faculty of Paris*, in *TT*, vol. 1 p. 110.

38. *The Necessity of Reforming the Church*, in *TT*, vol. 1, pp. 218f.

39. *Ibid.* p. 219.

40. Cf. *Confession of Faith in the Name of the Reformed Churches of France*, ch. 22, in *TT*, vol. 2, p. 150.

41. *Inst.* 4:7:26. On this whole section, see Rudolf J. Erlich, *Rome, Opponent or Partner?* pp. 225-230. Philadelphia: The Westminster Press, 1965.

42. *Brief Confession of Faith*, in *TT*, vol. 2, p. 134.

43. Auguste Sabatier, *Outlines of a Philosophy of Religion*, p. 218. London: 1906.

44. Stuart Louden, *The True Face of the Kirk*, p. 12. London: Oxford University Press, 1963.

45. Albert C. Outler, "A Response," in *The Documents of Vatican II*, ed. Walter M. Abbott, p. 104. New York: Guild Press, 1966.

46. "Ministry in the Church," A Statement by the Theology Section of the Roman Catholic/Presbyterian-Reformed Consultation, October 30, 1971, in *Journal of Ecumenical Studies*, vol. 9, no. 3 (Summer, 1972), pp. 589-612.

47. Philip Schaff, *The Principle of Protestantism as Related to the Present State of the Church*, ET by John W. Nevin, p. 174. Chambersburg, Pa.: German Reformed Church, 1845.

48. *Ibid.*, pp. 175-76.

49. *Bibliotheca Symbolica Ecclesiae Universalis, The Creeds of Christendom, with a History and Critical Notes*. New York & London: Harper and Brothers, 1877.

50. *Ibid.*, p. 170.

51. Philip Schaff, "The Reunion of Christendom," in *The World's Parliament of Religions*, ed. John Henry Barrows, vol. II, pp. 1195-96. Chicago: The Parliament Publishing Company, 1893. See James H. Smylie, "Philip Schaff: Ecumenist," in *Encounter*, vol. 28, no. 1 (Winter, 1967), pp. 3-16; also D. Bard Thompson, "The Mercersburg Divines," paper read before the Avon Literary Club, Mercersburg, Pennsylvania, May 4, 1962.

52. William Edwin Orchard, *Foundations of Faith*, vol. III, p. 47. New York: George H. Doran Company, 1926.

53. Raymond E. Brown, Karl P. Donfried, and John Reumann, eds., *Peter in the New Testament*. Minneapolis: Augsburg/New York: Paulist, 1973.

54. Hendrikus Berkhof, "A Protestant Viewpoint," in *The Future of Ecumenism*, ed. Hans Küng, pp. 122-126. Concilium, vol. 44, New York: Paulist Press, 1969.

Rome and Orthodoxy: Authority or Truth?

John Meyendorff

The Orthodox Church has always occupied a rather unusual place in the ecumenical dialogue which developed during
this century. This was perhaps inevitable, since the principal
concerns and basic presuppositions of the movement were
shaped by the historical features of *Western* Christianity in
their Roman Catholic and Protestant forms. However, the situation is currently undergoing a process of change, since the
concepts of "East" and "West," while retaining their significance in terms of theological tradition, have nevertheless lost
much of their geographical and cultural meaning. Though a
small minority, the Orthodox Church is now actively present in
traditionally Western countries, the United States particularly.
On the other hand, areas like Greece, the Balkans and Russia,
where Orthodox Christianity has long been predominant, also
belong to the "West" in a cultural sense, particularly if com-
pared to the newly emerging societies of Asia and Africa.

In this new environment, the ecclesiological issue which
traditionally separated Rome and Orthodoxy cannot be envisaged simply as a cultural phenomenon. If it could be reduced to such a simple question, it would probably disappear
as an issue. But even if one holds this "cultural" and purely
"historical" interpretation of the schism, and denies therefore
that any real theological and ecclesiological problem separates
the churches today, he should logically be compelled to pro-

duce a theologically and ecclesiologically sound working model of a "united church." But then the traditionally unavoidable issue of *authority* once again emerges as the central question, and one discovers that it cannot be solved without recourse to Scripture and tradition, for without the latter Christianity ceases to be Christ's and the Church is not the Church "of God."

During the past several years, relations between the Orthodox Church and Rome have gone through a series of quite extraordinary events, none of which could have been foreseen from the preceding generation, i.e., an exchange of documents "lifting the anathemas" of A.D. 1054, and several personal meetings between the pope and the patriarch of Constantinople. All of these events directly involve the question of authority, and especially *papal* authority, but none of them provide an articulate and definitive *solution* to the issue. The events were largely *symbolic* in nature: speeches, gestures and actions which changed the overall atmosphere. It is now the task of theologians to discover how these events can be interpreted and used, not for the narrow purpose of ecclesiastical diplomacy, or even the progress of "Orthodox-Catholic relations" (which is only one aspect of our responsibility for a united Christian witness), but for the solution of the problem of authority in the Church, without which no real Christian unity is possible.

In any case, because the Orthodox tradition on the question of authority is strikingly distinct from Western Christendom as a whole,[1] an Orthodox contribution to the present stage of the debate is crucially important.[2]

1. *The Schism: Two Ecclesiologies*

One of the most striking facts about the schism between the East and the West is that it cannot be *dated*. In the common declaration by Pope Paul and Patriarch Athenagoras published on December 7, 1965, the events of A.D. 1054 are reduced to their real (actually rather insignificant) proportions: "Among the obstacles which exist on the way toward the development of brotherly relations of confidence and esteem (between the churches), we find the remembrance of the decisions, acts and painful incidents which led, in A.D. 1054, to the sentence of excommunication published against Patriarch Michael Cerullarios and two other persons by the legates of the Roman see, headed by Cardinal Humbert; the legates were then subjected to a similar sentence issued by the synod of Constantinople. . . . We must recognize today that the sentences were directed at particular persons and not at the churches, and were not aiming at breaking ecclesial communion between the sees of Rome and Constantinople."[3]

It is clear from this text of the "lifting of the anathemas" that the authors were aware of the rather accidental character of the 1054 events. In 1054, no schism occurred between the churches as such. Humbert's text includes "the supporters of (Cerullarios') folly" under the condemnation but, in the same text, he considers the emperor of Constaninople and the citizens as "very Christian and orthodox." And in any case, his "bull" of excommunication exceeded his powers as legate, and was, apparently, null and void in the first place.

For Paul VI and Athenagoras, it was therefore rather easy to express "regret" about the "offensive words" of 1054 and "to lift from the memory and the midst of the Church the sentences of excommunication" of 1054, and it is good that they did so. However, they did not thereby put an end to the schism itself.

What, then, was the nature of the schism and when did it occur?

All historians admit today that East and West parted their ways through a *progressive* estrangement, which coincided with the equally *progressive* growth of papal authority. Theologians held centuries-long discussions on such issues as the trinitarian dogma (the *Filioque* question) and the issues were important ones. However, no solution of the debate could be reached until the two sides reached agreement not only on the substance of the questions which divided them (which was difficult enough), but also with regard to the authority which would ultimately sanction the agreement and on what basis.

Elements of the estrangement appeared in the fourth century, when a certain polarization in trinitarian theology had already existed for some time, as well as an incipient ecclesiological conflict. On the one hand, the West attributed a special authority to the so-called "apostolic sees" and recognized the Roman see as the only "see of Peter." In the East, on the other hand, "apostolic sees," i.e., local churches tracing their origin to an apostle, were so numerous that they could not from a practical standpoint pretend to any particular authority on that basis.[4] Leadership in the church was based on the *de facto* authority of certain sees; thus no one raised any objection of principle against the rise of the "ecumenical patriarchate" of Constantinople, the imperial capital, simply because of certain empirical factors quite independent of any "apostolicity."

Clearly, the ecclesiological polarization involved in this estrangement was connected with a gradually diverging understanding of the *local church*, i.e., the eucharistic community, headed by a bishop and presbyters and including the people of God. Relationships between the local churches were seen in the East to be based upon their *identity* of faith and total ontological equality, with "primacies" (metropolitanates, patriarchates, etc.) emerging on an empirical basis, conditioned and controlled only by the consensus of all the churches. In the West, the very insistence on "apostolicity" (particularly on the apostolicity of Rome alone, because it was the only "apostolic" see of the West) led to the idea of leadership by divine election, since Christ and not the Church had chosen and appointed the apostles and selected Peter for a special role in the Church. But when the debate started (actually not until the thirteenth century), the Byzantine side insisted upon the idea of a *succession of Peter in each local church* in the person of the bishop, the "high-priest" and teacher at the eucharistic gathering,[5] an idea already expressed in the doctrine of the *cathedra Petri* of St. Cyprian of Carthage in the third century.

The initial estrangement grew progressively deeper and was enhanced by political and cultural factors. If one excepts Pope Leo I and the important role his "Letter to Flavian" played at the Council of Chalcedon (A.D. 451), the Roman Church had no decisive influence upon the trinitarian and christological debates raging in the East. Its doctrinal prestige was acknowledged, but it was the conciliar agreement of the episcopate which was seen as the highest expression of ecclesial authority. This authority, however, was not juridically automatic, since there were many examples of "pseudo-councils." It belongs to the biblical category of divine "signs," addressed to the Christian community as a whole, without depriving it of its responsibility to "discern" truth and falsehood.

The Crusades, and particularly the attack on Constantinople which occurred in A.D. 1204, are frequently seen by historians as the real beginning of the schism. It is obvious, indeed, that establishment of a *parallel Latin hierarchy*, and particularly of a Latin patriarchate of Constantinople, put the schism in clear evidence. In any case, after the Gregorian reforms, the papacy considered itself as the only and ultimate authority in Christendom. Challenge to that authority was seen as a schismatic and heretical act. Faced with this clear-cut attitude, Easterners nevertheless maintained the idea that, in spite of all the crimes committed by the Crusaders, the Latin West remained a part of the Christian *oikoumene*, with whom some sort of arrangement must be made. This can be said not only of the "Latinophrones," who constantly pushed the weakening empire of the Palaeologi toward a "political" union with Rome in order to secure help against the Turks, but also of the more conservative Orthodox circles as well. These circles, which took theological issues quite seriously, and especially the addition of the *Filioque* to the Creed by the Latins, considered that a Council of union at which these differences would be openly debated and resolved was a necessary pre-condition for the healing of the schism.[6]

Throughout the fourteenth century, the debates between East and West centered around the idea of a Council. But was a Council to precede union, as the Byzantines wanted, or was an act of "penance," of "return," necessary as a pre-condition? The popes maintained the latter position until the papacy itself began to be challenged by the Conciliarist Movement of the West. Proclaiming the supremacy of the Council over the pope, the Council of Constance made the previously held papal position untenable and eventually led to a Council of union in Ferrara-Florence (1438-1439). Paradoxically, the Council of Florence ended in a double tragedy: the end of conciliarism in the West[7] and the final schism between the East and West. Indeed, the Decree of Florence,[8] by imposing upon an exhausted and despairing Greek delegation the traditional positions of the Latin West with regard to the *Filioque* question, purgatory and, last but not least, the definition of the Roman pontiff's position as implying "full power (*plena potestas*) to feed, rule and govern the universal Church," was bound to provoke a negative reaction. Most of the Greek delegates who signed the decree later denounced their signatures. The Church of Russia rejected Metropolitan Isidore, one of the architects of the union. The patriarchate of Constantinople, after the Turkish conquest, officially placed Latin Christians in the "second category" of heretics, to be accepted into the Church by Chrismation in accordance with canon 95, of the Quinisext Council (692).

All of these well-known events are to be kept in mind if the "lifting of anathemas" of 1965 is to be understood in its true light. Clearly, the end of the schism would require much more than this symbolic act and would imply in particular the acceptance by both sides of a common frame of reference in terms of Church *authority*.

There is, however, one major historical event which was indeed a significant achievement in terms of Church union, and if recognized as such today, could contribute substantially to solving the contradiction between the Eastern and Western understandings of authority. This event is the Council held in Constantinople in A.D. 879-880 to seal the reconciliation between Pope John VIII and Patriarch Photius. The reconciliation followed such ecclesiologically significant events as the mutual excommunications of Pope Nicholas I and Photius, and a first round of polemics concerning the *Filioque* clause.

Until recently it was assumed that Pope John VIII disavowed his legates when they returned from the East and that the schism continued. The work of Dvornik and other modern scholars has shown that this was not the case,[9] for not only Photius and John VIII, but their several successors remained faithful to the Council's decisions.

The Council's principal decisions were as follows:

1. On the level of discipline, the two churches recognized each other as supreme instances in their respective spheres: there would be no papal "jurisdiction" in the East (canon 1) but the traditional honorary primacy of Rome would be recognized, as well as the traditional territorial limits of the Roman patriarchate.

2. On the level of doctrinal teaching, the Council maintains unity of faith, through a reaffirmation of the original text of the Creed of Nicea-Constantinople; "additions" to the text are explicitly condemned. The *Filioque* is clearly implied in the conciliar decree, but the authority of the pope is not directly involved, since the addition at that time was not yet used in Rome itself, but only in Frankish countries and in Spain.

What is the significance of these decisions?

The texts themselves call the Council "holy and ecumenical." And indeed all the criteria of ecumenicity, accepted for previous councils, were present in 879-880 (imperial convocation, representation of the five patriarchates, including Rome). In Byzantine canonical collections, the decrees of 879-880 always follow those of the other seven ecumenical Councils. Byzantine authors often mention the assembly as the "eighth" ecumenical Council. This is the case, for example, with such eminent and representative authors as Nicholas Cabasilas[10] and Symeon of Thessalonica.[11] But this usage is not general; some Byzantine authors considered the "seven Councils" as *de facto* limited in number by the sacredness of the number seven! Others respected the Latin reticences concerning the Council.

In the West, meanwhile, as Dvornik shows,[12] the Council of 879-880 was recognized, if not as ecumenical, then at least as a competent authority, sanctioned by Rome, which did in fact re-establish Church unity by annulling the previously held "Ignatian" Council (869-870) which had deposed Photius.[13] Only the "Gregorian reform" at the end of the eleventh century restored the authority of the "Ignatian" Council. The Gregorian reforms recognized themselves in the *Acts* of this Council which (so they thought) affirmed the authority of the pope over the Byzantine patriarch and the civil power of the emperors. But, between 880 and 1100, i.e., for more than two centuries, the East and the West in spite of the other differences which separated them recognized the legitimacy of the agreement between John VIII and Photius which was sealed at St. Sophia in 880.

Clearly, the rather tardy introduction of the Ignatian Council of 869-870 in the list of "ecumenical" Councils does present the Roman concept of authority with a problem. Can it be reconciled with such an obvious case of discontinuity? It is interesting, however, that at least once the issue was successfully by-passed. During the fourth and fifth sessions of the Council in Ferrara, on October 20 and 24, A.D. 1438, Cardinal Cesarini and Andrew of Rhodes, the main spokesmen for the Latin side, invoked the authority of the "eighth Council," meaning the Ignatian Council of 869-870. They immediately had to face a blunt *Non possumus* of Mark of Ephesus, the Greek spokesman, who expressly appealed to the formal annulment of this Council under Pope John VIII.[14] By common accord, the ticklish issue was buried and the Council of Florence became the "eighth" Council. The Latin side thus implicitly accepted a return to the situation which preceded the Gregorian reform.

This brings us to an idea which in my opinion might solve, perhaps decisively, the problem of authority between Rome and Orthodoxy: Would it not be possible for both churches today *to recognize jointly the Photian Council of 879-880 as ecumenical?*

An action of this nature would certainly go much farther than the purely symbolic "lifting of the anathemas" of 1054. It would imply the return to a situation of ecumenical unity which existed for more than two centuries, i.e., from A.D. 880-1100. For the Orthodox such an action would require the agreement of all the local Orthodox churches and would mean that union is really based on identity of faith, expressed in the common creed. For tradition-minded Rome, it would not be a simple abdication of authority, but a return to a situation solemnly sanctioned by a predecessor of the present pope.

The nature of the schism being what it is, it is clear that symbolic gestures and ceremonial meetings are quite insufficient to overcome the existing division. What is needed is a union of minds and a basic agreement on institutional forms of unity. The Council of 879-880 accomplished both.

2. *What Happened in the Sixties?*

We have described the various statements and encounters between the pope and the patriarch of Constantinople which took place in the sixties as having been essentially of a *symbolic* nature. As all symbols, these can be wrongly interpreted. It has been said, for example, that the spectacular character of the encounters and the ambiguity of the documents gave the mistaken impression that union was imminent and that doctrinal obstacles existed only in the minds of a few reactionary theologians. It has also been said that the ecclesiastical diplomacy which prepared and subsequently effected the encounters was aimed at projecting the false image of an Orthodox "papacy," parallel to the Roman one. In this regard, it must be conceded that an uninformed Western public opinion may have occasionally considered the ecumenical patriarch to be the Eastern equivalent of a pope. On the Orthodox side, meanwhile, the skeptics found consolation in the fact that the patriarch was not invested with any official pan-Orthodox mandate and that he was neither speaking nor acting for the whole church.

It would be unfortunate, however, if these critiques of the papal and patriarchal diplomacies (though sometimes justified) were to neutralize completely the real importance of certain words and gestures. The events may still bring about results which transcend our immediate reactions. It would be impossible, for example, even to think about a joint acceptance of the Council of 879-880 if the atmosphere created by Vatican II as well as the meetings between Paul VI and Athenagoras was not with us.

In this connection, there are two realities which merit particular attention, because they are directly relevant to the central issue of authority.

(1) The public *image* of a pope appearing in Istanbul and in Rome as a *brother* (and therefore ontologically an *equal*) of another bishop cannot be reduced to mere diplomacy or protocol. The well-known definitions of papal supremacy were in no way denounced, of course, but neither were they publicly expressed in any way. Facing the Orthodox, the pope presented himself in a way perfectly compatible with the function of *primus inter pares* ("first among equals") which the Orthodox had recognized in him in the past. This attitude of Paul VI reversed a thousand-year-old tradition which required that the authority of the supreme pontiff be scrupulously preserved under any circumstances, and particularly in his relations with the East, where the existence of a center of opposition to Roman centralism was a well-known fact.

The rupture of that tradition is evident in the case of Pope Paul, and it raises a general ecclesiological question: Isn't there a contradiction between the fraternal embrace exchanged with Athenagoras, whose episcopal dignity, magisterial authority and patriarchal jurisdiction were strictly independent of Rome, and the power exercised by the pope over the Latin episcopate, a power which is traditionally justified by the notion of a "universal jurisdiction" by divine right? It appears (at least to this author) that papal power as defined by Vatican I is either universal, or it is not. It is difficult to understand why the bishops of France, Polynesia, America or Africa would benefit from a divinely established papal "immediate" jurisdiction, while the bishops of Greece, Russia or the Middle East would not.

There are still no clear answers to these questions, and perhaps these answers would be difficult to conceptualize. At the same time, it is also apparent that a diversity of trends and a variety of pressure groups exist inside Roman Catholicism. Paradoxically, however, those groups which are most opposed to Roman centralism are not always sympathetic to the values represented by Orthodoxy: faithfulness to apostolic doctrine and a sacramental approach to Church polity. The fact remains, nevertheless, that the pope and patriarch sitting side by side and addressing each other as equals has established a precedent which needs a theological and ecclesial reception and interpretation. In other words, the symbol needs to be given a substantial content.

(2) On July 25, 1967, in Istanbul, the pope handed to Patriarch Athenagoras the brief *Anno ineunte*, which attempted to express the relationship between Rome and Constantinople by using the traditional Orthodox concept of "sister churches." The text recognized that the term is appropriate to describe the relations as they existed "for centuries," and then it continues: "Now, after a long period of division and reciprocal misunderstanding, it occurs, by the grace of God, that our Churches recognize each other as sisters once more."[15] The basis for such a recognition is found in the mystery of the sacramental presence of Christ. This mystery is present in each local church, and therefore "communion (between our churches), though imperfect, already exists."

(a) This text seems to imply that the rapproachement between East and West must be understood as a *progressive mutual recognition of local churches*, and not as a return to Roman "obedience." It is certain that this method basically corresponds to the Orthodox approach to the ecumenical task in general, with the understanding that rapprochement with Rome possesses a much more solid ecclesiological basis for the Orthodox than its ecumenical contacts with the Protestants. The question arises, however, whether this method can be really consistent with those definitions of Roman primacy which are based on the exclusive "Petrine" ministry of the pope. In fact, at the very beginning of the brief *Anno ineunte* itself the pope is designated as "bishop of the Roman Church and head of the universal Church,"[16] a title which clearly reflects an ecclesiology which the Orthodox consider as quite incompatible with their own. Isn't there a contradiction in the brief itself?

(b) The brief also implies that the doctrinal definitions made by the Latin Church and traditionally rejected by the Orthodox, i.e., the addition of the *Filioque* to the text of the Creed, the decrees of the Council of Trent, and the dogma of the Immaculate Conception of Mary (1854), are somehow parenthesized. Their rejection by the Orthodox does not therefore preclude "an almost full" communion. This implication of the brief *Anno ineunte* has recently been reinforced by the text of a letter of Pope Paul VI to Cardinal Willebrands, dated October 5, 1974. The cardinal was the papal legate at the celebrations of the 700th anniversary of the Council of Lyons (1274), which solemnly defined the theology of the *Filioque* and accepted the Unionist confession of faith signed by the Byzantine emperor Michael VIII Palaeologus. The most remarkable aspect of this papal letter is its recognition that the Council gave no "possibility to the Greek Church of expressing itself freely" and that "a unity achieved in this way could not be accepted completely by the mentality of the Eastern Christians." Even more significantly, the pope calls the Council of Lyons "the sixth of the General Synods held in the Western world," and *not* an "ecumenical Council." Can the same therefore be said of Trent, Vatican I and Vatican II? If so, a really important step seems to have been taken, modifying the previously held concept of papal authority.

In any case, the texts seem to imply that the Latin

dogmas, so solemnly proclaimed in the past, should not be considered as possessing a universal validity, and therefore would not constitute an obstacle to union. If this is really so, the authority of the Roman Church, which previously committed itself so heavily behind these dogmas, should also be seen in a new light. On the other hand, a canonical and sacramental union which would not presuppose the solution of the problems raised by these Latin definitions would raise even more acutely the whole question of theological pluralism in a united Church.

Certainly, there is nothing new in considering certain practices and doctrines as *theologoumena*, i.e., positions taken by individual theologians without formal ecclesial sanction. Liturgical and theological pluralism are both unavoidable and desirable in the one Church. But this admissible pluralism is not an end in itself, and should not be used to justify doctrinal relativism as such, or to cover up serious doctrinal conflicts. A *theologoumenon* cannot be imposed as obligatory doctrine, but everyone has the right to reject it if he sees it as erroneous. The later Latin dogmas would certainly be seen in this last category by the Orthodox: they were not only signs of pluralism, but occasions for century-old conflicts. Can one have unity without solving these problems first?

Another set of questions raised by texts like *Anno ineunte* and the papal letter to Cardinal Willebrands is also directly connected with the issue of authority. The texts certainly make a positive step in the direction of the Orthodox if they really imply that Latin medieval and modern doctrinal developments are not obligatory for the Easterners, because the Eastern "sister churches" did not in fact receive them. But if these doctrines failed to obtain the support of the East, does this not mean that they should be treated with at least some reservations in the West as well? Can the authority of doctrinal definitions, e.g., at Lyons, Florence, Trent, and Vatican I, be limited geographically? On the other hand, the Orthodox certainly should feel some responsibility for the West as well, where some of these "dogmas" have also provoked conflicts. And finally, what is the "East" and what is the "West" in 1975?

The remarkable change of atmosphere witnessed recently in the relations between the two churches, in addition to the very real efforts made by Popes John XXIII and Paul VI to meet the Orthodox on the question of Church authority, surely requires a balanced theological evaluation to indicate whether the questions raised above have received at least the beginning of an answer.

3. *The Ambiguity of the Present Situation*

The question of authority has stood for centuries in the very center of the issues between East and West. Writing in the middle of the last century, the Russian lay theologian A. S. Khomyakov defined the issue in the form of a rather romantic overstatement, which nevertheless remains quite revealing today: "The Church is not an authority, just as God is not an authority and Christ is not an authority, since authority is something external to us. The Church is not an authority, I say, but the Truth, and at the same time the inner life of the Christian, since God, Christ, the Church, live in him with a life more real than the heart which is beating in his breast and the blood flowing in his veins. But they are alive in him only insofar as he himself is living by the ecumenical life of love and unity, i.e., by the life of the Church." Khomyakov's main reproach to the West is that it has transformed authority into external power: the *magisterium* in Roman Catholicism, Scripture in Protestantism; in both cases, he concludes, "the premises are identical."[17]

Khomyakov's notion of an "internal" knowledge of the Truth, independent of "external" criteria and authorities, would be pure romantic subjectivism if read outside of the context of Greek patristic understanding of God and man. For the Greek Fathers, knowledge of God is based on the notion of communion and the transfiguration and deification of man; it implies the theory of the "spiritual senses," i.e., an utterly personal experience of the living God, made accessible through the sacramental, communal life in the body of Christ.[18] This gnosiology does not suppress "authorities" and "criteria," but these are clearly *internal* to the Christian experience; they furnish an authentication which is incomprehensible to anyone who has not first personally accepted its validity and tasted the reality of the experience itself.

The experience is that of Truth itself, not simply of any means of attaining the truth. The divine presence of God in man through the Holy Spirit is "uncreated." It is the Truth therefore that authenticates authority, and not the opposite. It is precisely this understanding of authority which made the East resist so stubbornly against acceptance of the institution of papacy as the criterion of Truth, and to reaffirm so consistently that it is the faith of Peter which conditions primacy, while primacy itself is not a guarantee of infallibility. This is, in fact, the traditional issue between Rome and Orthodoxy, which can in no way be identified as a purely *cultural* difference between "East" and "West." Even if some of the formal doctrinal definitions accepted in Roman Catholicism and rejected in Orthodoxy were to be seen only as Western *theologoumena*, i.e., points of an agenda for a future joint Council, it is clear that the two central affirmations of Vatican I, i.e., papal infallibility *ex sese, non ex consensu Ecclesiae* ("of itself and not resulting from the consensus of the Church") and the pope's "immediate" and "truly episcopal" jurisdiction over all the faithful, would unavoidably call into question the basis for the future Council itself. Vatican II is in fact quite specific on this point:

The college or body of bishops has no authority unless it is simultaneously conceived of in terms of its head, the Roman pontiff, Peter's successor, and without any lessening of his power of primacy over all, pastors as well as the general faithful. For in virtue of his office, that is, as vicar of Christ and pastor of the whole Church, the Roman pontiff has full, supreme, and universal power over the Church. And he can always exercise this power freely.[19]

Together with the other passages where Vatican Council II takes pains to point out that none of the papal privileges as defined in 1870 are diminished by the new emphasis on "episcopal collegiality," this text clearly shows that not only collegiality, but even the individual *exercise* of the episcopate by any bishop (except the pope himself) is placed under the pope's power and is at his discretion.[20] Episcopal collegiality is always seen as depending upon the pope, but the reverse is not true: the pope is not dependent upon the bishops in the exercise of his primatial ministry, and the faithful are required to show "religious submission of will and of mind . . . to the authentic teaching authority of the Roman pontiff, even when he is not speaking *ex cathedra*."[21]

Thus the otherwise remarkable effort made by Vatican II to integrate the papacy into an ecclesiological context which would be closer to that of the early Church has not succeeded in removing the real issue between Orthodoxy and Rome. Inasmuch as the texts of Vatican II still affirm that the pope is the ultimate *criterion* of Christian truth, with all the other authorities being subsidiary to his, the moves made recently by Rome toward the concept of "sister churches" and toward limiting the significance of the unilateral decisions of the past are not devoid of ambiguity. Or is there a clear contradiction, and is it deliberate?

Without attempting to answer these difficult questions, it seems important to point out that there is an even more tragic ambiguity in the situation of Western Christianity resulting from the Council. It appears, in fact, that centuries of authoritarian religion have conditioned some people's minds and habits so much that authority seems at times to be the only means of maintaining basic Christian truths. In this respect, Orthodox Christians behave differently; because they feel themselves *responsible* for the truth, they are naturally rather suspicious of authority, even when it suggests useful reforms. Freedom thus leads to conservatism. On the contrary, the traditional reliance of Western Christianity upon authority in matters of religion creates a religious void wherever authority weakens or disappears. Deprived of the security provided by the familiar authority structures (the teaching Church, or the inerrant Bible), and suspicious of anything which was associated with it (including paradoxically the liturgical mystery), Western Christianity appears to move in directions which estrange it most from Orthodoxy: humanistic activism and secularism. But then, as a reaction against these trends, the old clerical forms of post-Tridentine Roman Catholicism and conservative Protestant fundamentalism reappear, stronger than ever.

Clearly, all this may be seen as an oversimplification. But it does reflect the feeling of many Orthodox whose reaction is to withdraw from the ecumenical "adventures" altogether and simply to enjoy on their own the beautiful foretaste of the Kingdom to come in the Orthodox liturgy, due to their inability to identify with either pole of contemporary Western Christianity.

It is certainly not my intention to finish on such a pessimistic note for I do not believe that withdrawal from dialogue is anything but a renunciation of one's "catholic" responsibility. But I would emphasize the fact that between the conciliar ecclesiology of Orthodoxy and the infallibilism of Rome, the issue is indeed that of "authority." Since the sixties, however, the issue can be seen in a new dimension, for any discussion of papal primacy and Church authority in general has become impossible without relating it to the very *content* of the Christian Gospel.

Is an infallible papacy a part of this content? To answer this question positively is, for an Orthodox, an authentic aberration ultimately responsible not only for the schism between East and West but also, indirectly, for so much superficiality and irresponsibility in approaching the problem of Truth! The fact that so many people lose their commitment to the basic Christian revelation as soon as it ceases to be "guaranteed" in human terms, through the deprivation of the false security of authoritarianism, measures the dimension of the tragedy. This reality was so well understood and expressed by St. Paul in Galatians 4 and by Dostoyevsky in his *Legend of the Great Inquisitor*.

The problem, then, cannot be met with superficial canonical adjustments or ecumenical double-talk. What is needed is no less than a recovery of the "mind of Christ" so that "we might know the things that are freely given to us by God" (1 Cor. 2:12, 16).

NOTES

1. On this particular issue see John Meyendorff, *Orthodoxy and Catholicity*, New York, Sheed and Ward, 1966, pp. 119-140; and, by the same author, the article "Historical Relativism and Authority in Christian Dogma" in the *Jurist*, 1971:1, Studies in Church Law and Ministry, Washington, D.C., 1971, pp. 143-162.

2. The ideas in this chapter were first developed in the preparation for a talk given on March 28, 1974 in Vienna, Austria at the center *Pro Oriente*.

3. *Tomos Agapes*, Vatican-Phanar (1958-1970); Rome, Istanbul, 1971, p. 127.

4. This point is brilliantly shown in F. Dvornik, *The Legend of the Apostle Andrew and the Idea of Apostolicity in Byzantium*, Cambridge, Mass., 1958.

5. On this dimension of Orthodox ecclesiology, see J. D. Zizioulas, "The Eucharistic Community and the Catholicity of the Church" in J. Meyendorff and J. McLelland, eds., *The New Man—An Orthodox and Reformed Dialogue*, Agora Books, New Brunswick, N.J., 1973, pp. 132-148; also on the idea of Peter's succession in Byzantium, J. Meyendorff *et al.*, eds., *The Primacy of Peter in the Orthodox Church*, London, Faith Press, 1963.

6. See J. Meyendorff, "Projets de concile oecumenique en 1367" in *Dumbarton Oaks Papers* 14 (1960).

7. Cf. J. Gill, *The Council of Florence*, Cambridge, 1959, p. vii.

8. H. Denzinger and C. Rahner, *Enchiridion Symbolorum*, Freiburg, 1952, pp. 252-253.

9. See particularly F. Dvornik, *The Photian Schism: History and Legend*, Cambridge, 1948.

10. Preamble to the works of Nilus Cabasilas, PG 149, col. 679.

11. *Dial.* 19, PG 155, col. 97.

12. *Op. cit.*, pp. 309-330.

13. In a recent book Daniel Stiernon tries to re-establish the authority of this "Ignatian Council" which is listed as "eighth ecumenical" in the presently accepted Roman Catholic lists (*Constantinople IV*, Paris, Editions de l'Orante, 1967, pp. 199-230). But the famous *Decree* of Ivo of Chartres, published in 1094, witnesses unquestionably to the rehabilitation of Photius by John VIII, as it was then recognized in the West.

14. *Concilium Florentinum. Documenta et Scriptores, Series B.* Vol. V, fasc. I, *Acta Graeca*, Rome, 1952, pp. 90-91, 135.

15. *Tomos Agapes*, p. 390.

16. To avoid embarrassing the Orthodox, the Greek text of the brief translates *caput* ("head") as *hegoumenos* ("leader"). This diplomatic mistranslation only emphasizes the ambiguity of the thought lying behind the text of the brief.

17. *Quelques mots d'un chrétien orthodoxe sur les confessions occidentales*, Paris, 1853; reprinted in *L'Eglise latine et le protestantisme au point de vue de l'Eglise d'Orient. Recueil d'articles sur des questions religieuses ecrits à différents époques et à différentes occasions*, Lausanne et Vevey, 1872, pp. 36-37; Engl. tr. in A. Schmemann, ed., *Ultimate Questions*, Holt, Rinehart and Winston, New York, 1965, pp. 50-51.

18. The classical book on Eastern Christian gnosiology is by V. Lossky, *The Mystical Theology of the Eastern Church*, London: Clarke, 1957; see also, by the same author, *Vision of God*, London: Faith Press, 1963, and J. Meyendorff, *Byzantine Theology: Historical Trends and Doctrinal Themes*, New York, Fordham University Press, 1974.

19. Vatican II, "Dogmatic Constitution on the Church," III, 22, in W. Abbott, ed., *The Documents of Vatican II*, Guild Press, New York, 1966, p. 43.

20. Cf. our commentary on these texts in *Orthodoxy and Catholicity*, Sheed and Ward, New York, 1966, pp. 150-165.

21. Vatican II, "Dogmatic Constitution on the Church," III, 25, *ed. cit.*, p. 48.

Methodism and the Papacy

J. Robert Nelson

I

THE TRADITION AND EXERCISE
OF AUTHORITY IN METHODISM

Methodism is usually catalogued among the "free churches" of Anglo-American Christianity. Why free? Not because it is without an authoritative polity or lacking in authoritarian leaders. The idea of a "free church" can properly pertain to two aspects of Methodism. First, it sprang from and departed from the established Church of England, joining other nonconformist denominations of that land. And second, Methodism has been and remains free from the strict requirements of a single doctrinal confession and liturgical pattern. These are significant kinds of freedom, the first relating only to British experience, the second to Methodists everywhere. But to rank Methodism among such "free church" bodies as Baptists, Congregationalists or Mennonites is inappropriate. From the beginning of the eighteenth century until now the Methodist movement and its churches have been bound by the principle of strong authority, and Methodists are quite used to experiencing it in practice.

John Wesley, the originator and patriarch of Methodism, was small of stature but gigantic in achievement and formidable in leadership. The methodical discipline of the "Holy Club" of students at Oxford developed into a stern rule for the devoted members of the "societies" and "classes" which were formed. Wesley not only exemplified the adherence to daily discipline but expected it of all the men and women in the movement. When he convened the first "conference" of his preachers in 1744, he wanted of the Methodists nothing other than the daily expression of "scriptural holiness" as befits those who are "going on to perfection" in this life. Faithful Anglican priest that he was, he entertained no thought of organizing a new church. He urged his rapidly growing numbers of followers to attend the parish churches every Lord's Day for the Holy Communion, worshiping as Anglicans. But as Methodists they participated in the small "classes" for mutual edification and encouragement, and received the nourishment of the Gospel as proclaimed by Wesley's band of preachers.

Some of the preachers were ordained presbyters, or priests, of the Church of England; some were laymen. Wesley believed that they should move frequently from place to place with their evangelistic mission, rather than settle in a rectory. He was himself the most itinerant of preachers. His inimitable Journal shows that he was almost constantly on horseback, visiting all parts of the British Isles. His saddlebag was both desk and bookcase. And he required a similar, though reduced, itinerancy for all preachers.

Wesley reserved—some would say, arrogated—to himself the power to decide on the "circuits" which the preachers would serve. Circuits were, and still are, composed of "preaching stations" and after two centuries the ordained Methodists are often still designated "traveling elders." The phrase reminds one of the "journeyman printer" and connotes the mobility and vitality of Wesley's polity. So the 1972 edition of *The Book of Discipline*, which amounts to canon law for The United Methodist Church, asserts: "The itinerant system is the accepted method . . . by which ministers are appointed by the bishop to fields of labor."[1] The prototype of the present bishop is Wesley himself.

Defending himself in 1766 against certain critics, Wesley declared that as early as 1738 (the year of his famous heart-warming conversion) he had assumed "the power to appoint when and where and how they (the preachers) should meet; and to remove those whose life showed that they had no desire to flee from the wrath to come. And this power," he added, "remained the same, whether the people meeting together were twelve, twelve hundred, or twelve thousand."[2] As the historian Thomas B. Neely reflected: "Wesley exercised great power, but he exerted his authority with great wisdom and consideration. . . . He was the absolute head, and yet he was not a despot who had seized or usurped authority, but was the free choice of both members and ministers. He was the supreme government."[3] That Wesley was the "free choice" did not mean that he had been elected to his position by majority vote or appointed by a representative body of people. He was their choice because they accepted his obvious gift for spiritual and temporal leadership.

Under the historical circumstances of Methodism's beginnings there was no need for Wesley to establish his position by appeal to past traditions or biblical warrant. He was the once-for-all overseer of "the people called Methodists" in both Britain and America. In this role he resembled the mysterious priest Melchizedek, having neither predecessor nor successor. Although he had wanted and even designated a successor in the person of the admirable Swiss immigrant, John Fletcher, Wesley in his old age could not convince the Methodists that anyone was capable of continuing his authoritative position. So the actual successor to Wesley proved to be, not a person, but the Conference of preachers. The Methodist movement then became a church in both a sociological and a legal sense. In Great Britain today it is the Conference which exercises oversight and authority, these being invested in no particular offices. The president of the Conference is elected annually, but he scarcely can be said to represent a primacy of power.

The formation in America of a Methodist *Episcopal* Church was hardly less spontaneous and undetermined than the appearance of Wesley's personal rule in the home country. In neither case did the Methodists begin by agreeing to form a new church body and then undertake a study of the Scriptures and the tradition to determine what optimum form and polity it should have. The Church of England, which was their matrix, had not done this in the sixteenth century, but had simply imposed modifications upon its Roman Catholic predecessor with which it claimed continuity. Presbyterians had followed scrupulously the biblical and historical scholarship of John Calvin, in whose *Institutes of the Christian Religion* the structure and ministry of the church were sharply defined. But Methodist polity was a pragmatic application to the given situation of conceptions and practices which were already familiar, or which seemed expedient, to the people.

After the War of Independence, American Methodists were ecclesial orphans. Wesley had always insisted on their being communicants of Anglican churches. In the 1780's such churches, now identified with Toryism, were in disrepute and were actually without a bishop. How could there be services of Holy Communion or ordinations of ministers to preside over them? Wesley met the crisis in 1784 with a bold and controversial act: he himself ordained two men as presbyters and set apart as superintendent for America another ordained Anglican, Thomas Coke. It should not be thought that Wesley's power had gone to his head so that he fancied himself equal to a bishop and thus empowered to ordain. It was not such a conceit, but rather it was careful biblical study with the help of notable books by Anglican divines which had convinced him years before that the New Testament draws no clear line of distinction between *presbuteros* and *episkopos*. In accord with Calvinism in the past and with twentieth-century biblical scholarship of the future, Wesley believed himself to be both presbyter and bishop. Even as he once wrote that he had gone "unwillingly" to his Aldersgate experience of conversion in 1738, so his ordinations of 1784 were done with reluctance. However, due to the circumstances, he said that he felt "providentially called" to perform them.

On Christmas Eve of that same year, in the city of Baltimore, the preachers gathered under the leadership of Thomas Coke and Francis Asbury to constitute a church in the full legal sense. Using the structure of the Church of England as a model, and being uninhibited by the presence of any Anglican bishops in the new nation, they agreed upon an episcopal form of ministry and government. The aged Wesley back in England was still acknowledged as the authoritative leader, but his judgment upon the new church was ambiguous. That is, he approved the episcopal form but discouraged the use of the title "bishop" for Coke and Asbury. Despite Wesley's mordant letter of disapproval, however, the two men accepted both the role and the title of bishop. They even used the words "ordained" and "ordination" with respect to their becoming bishops, thus implying but not justifying the acceptance of episcopacy as a third order of ministry along with the orders of deacon and presbyter. For nearly two centuries, therefore, American Methodists have been undecided whether the bishop is only a "general superintendent" or "presiding elder" or a member of a special order of ministry. For most people, it has not been a problem of any gravity. Bishops are taken for granted; their official power and authority are accepted; and the personalities of the bishops have contributed as much as almost anything to the reality of their supervising authority. The word "almost" is needed to take account of the essential prerogative of the bishop, patterned after Wesley's: namely, his power of appointing ministers to their "charges" or parishes. The question of the identity or special character of the bishop, or of his order, as a theological matter has become important only in the ventures of recent years to seek church unions involving episcopal churches of the Anglican Communion. Therefore, the related question of the spiritual authority of the episcopal office, beyond the administrative, is relatively new.

The impression should not be gained by the preceding discussion that Methodist bishops, of whatever denomination, are just hierarchical autocrats. Many have no doubt given that impression by the style of their dealing with ministers and laity under their supervision. But at least an equal number or more have exhibited modesty and restraint. The important constitutional fact is that the bishops do not make up the governing body of the church. (Hereafter it is The United Methodist Church which we are discussing.) To explore the meaning of constitutional authority, we turn from this brief historical survey to examine the polity of the church as contained in *The Book of Discipline.*

If "collegiality" is a relatively new word for Methodists, the idea is as old as Methodism. The equivalent term is "conference." This word is the key to the Methodist understanding of ecclesial authority. It has a virtually canonical status. It is not merely an organizational device. Even though the theological rationale for the conference has not been so clarified and systematized as to be accorded a doctrinal value, the belief in the integrity of this form of collegiality is implicit in the corporate life of Methodism.

John Wesley's original yearly conference in 1744 has developed into a complex and inclusive system. Within it are seen the everyday operations of the church's principles of authority. There are five levels of conference:

1. The *General Conference* has "full legislative power over all matters distinctively connectional." It meets every four years with up to one thousand delegates from the annual conferences. One-half of the delegates are laity, one-half ordained ministers. During a period of two weeks the conference deliberates on matters pertaining to the whole church, enacts legislation, defines policies, and adopts quadrennial programs.

2. The *Jurisdictional Conference* is also quadrennial. There are five of these in the United States. Essentially considered, the business of these conferences is to elect bishops as vacancies occur by retirement or death. The balloting is preferential, without prior nominations. Both laity and clergy vote.

3. The *Annual Conference*, while subordinate in authority to the first two, is called by *The Discipline* "the basic body of

the church." This is because the implementation of all church life which is "connectional" (another distinctive Wesleyan word) takes place here. Within the connection of the annual conference are diverse numbers of local churches, ranging from about forty to a thousand. Even though beholden to the General Conference, the annual conferences retain the power of amending the very Constitution under which the General Conference operates.

4. The *District Conference* comprises a smaller number of local churches in a portion of a large city or in one or more counties of a rural area. Its purpose is mainly programmatic.

5. The *Charge Conference*, meeting annually, includes representative members and office-holders of the local congregation, or of some clusters of small congregations served by the same minister.

For most Methodists the only dimension of this pentagonal conference structure which they know by experience is the local one, the pastoral charge. Without being aware of it as a theological reality, they affirm that the wholeness, or catholicity, of the church finds its expression in the local community —a conviction held since ancient times by the Eastern Orthodox, for a long while by the Congregationalists and Baptists, and recently emphasized in a different way by Roman Catholics such as Karl Rahner.[4]

If these conferences may be said to constitute the parts of the denomination's body, then the connecting tissues are the bishops, their assistants (called district superintendents), and the executive officers of national agencies.

The authority and function of the episcopate in Methodism cannot be likened exactly to that of either the Roman Catholic or the Protestant Episcopal Church. Few Methodists, for example, are concerned with the ecumenically significant question of whether their bishops stand in the historic apostolic succession. The fact is that no such claim is made for them. The succession is of highest importance for Orthodoxy and Catholicism, of course, and for a great many Anglicans. But a prominent Methodist bishop was probably expressing the cavalier view of most of his colleagues when he said that he would gladly accept a ritual form of admission to the apostolic succession for the sake of church unity—and would regard it as similar to receiving an honorary degree!

The function of the bishop is far more important in practice than the question of his order or his episcopal character. Even so, there have developed many outward and visible signs of an inward penchant for traditional Catholic and Anglican episcopacy in Methodism. In matters of dress and adornment, the amethyst ring and the purple clerical stock are often worn, and the affecting of a purple cassock is not unknown. Without referring to episcopal succession, the Constitution nevertheless prescribes that bishops' consecration (does it equal ordination?) shall be "in the historic manner." Though the manner is left undefined, this means in effect that at least three other bishops participate in the laying on of hands. Why? In The United Methodist Church the tenure and identity of the bishop are for his lifetime, but some other Methodist churches have term episcopacy of four years subject to further election. Moreover, in Methodism it is the bishops who ordain others to deacon's and elder's order, but they do not confirm the baptized members.

When considered in the Western episcopal tradition, then, the exact identity and authorization of the Methodist bishop are not clearly defined.

As for the bishop's practical function, however, there is no mystery or secret. With respect to general administrative power and responsibility it is often observed that the Roman Catholic counterpart is not the bishop, but the archbishop. It is the district superintendent, appointed by the bishop for usually a six-year term, whose Catholic analogue is the diocesan bishop. The Methodist bishop has charge of an "area" which may include one to four annual conferences. He presides over sessions of the annual conferences and has executive responsibility for the whole program of the conferences. Every bishop, moreover, holds one or more positions of national responsibility, such as being chairman of a program agency or standing committee.

The member of another episcopal-type church who reads *The Discipline* is no doubt disappointed in the total lack of any theological or historical warrant for episcopacy, and also by the ten "duties and powers" which are assigned to the bishop. Except for a general duty of overseeing "the spiritual and temporal affairs of the Church," the bishop apparently has only administrative work to do. Nothing is said about the bishop's ministry as made familiar in recent ecumenical discussions of the office. Is the bishop *pastor pastorum*? Is the bishop a guardian of "the faith once delivered to the saints," and hence a teacher? Is the bishop a sacramental figure, a eucharistic leader? Does the bishop symbolize the unity of the whole church on earth in time as well as space? One does not have to be a critical non-Methodist to miss the statement of such conceptions. This is why, at the time of writing in 1975, a denominational study on the meaning of episcopacy is in progress. And it is clear that a number of bishops who have been influenced by ecumenical relations are reconsidering the nature of their office.

If the previous paragraph seems to be rather negative, there are some positive features about Methodist polity and practice as these touch upon the authority of the bishop. These might well be considered in the ecumenical discussion of authority and primacy.

First should be mentioned the fact that each quadrennium the bishop's "character and official administration" are reviewed by the jurisdictional conference which elected him. The review is done by a committee composed of both laity and elders, which also must make a recommendation on the appointment of the bishop for another four-year period. This is quite an unusual, even astonishing, example of broad collegiality in church affairs.

Second, when the General Conference meets, the sixty or so active bishops are allowed no vote in the proceedings, and they may speak only when called upon—unless sitting in the presiding officer's chair.

A third balance to episcopal power is the body called the Council on Ministries. Established in 1972 by the General Conference, this large unit enjoying broad powers was labeled by its critical detractors "the Methodist curia." The analogy is not quite apt. But the bishops were also apprehensive about it, because it appeared that their prerogatives were being challenged dangerously. All the bishops together belong to the Council of Bishops, for which the Constitution makes provision. This council has obviously exhibited a concentration of ecclesiastical power, which the Constitution describes in broadest terms. So when the 1972 General Conference interposed the new Council on Ministries, representing a cross-section of the whole membership, the bishops felt moved to make an appeal to the highest juridical level in this church, which thus far has not been mentioned. It is the Judicial Council, which is elected by the General Conference and is empowered to make decisions categorically and without possibility of appeal. This bears striking resemblance to the Supreme Court of the United States, consisting of nine persons: four laity and five clergy—but no bishops! Taking these three councils together, then, it was the decision of the Judicial Council that the powers of the Council on Ministries did not infringe upon the proper powers of the Council of Bishops.

There is a fourth council which none but the unsophisticated would fail to mention in this analysis and description of the church. It is the Council on Finance and Administration, which obviously has the ancient power of the purse. It is amenable directly to the General Conference. Efforts in 1972 to require it to be responsible to the Council on Ministries were thwarted. And, of course, in the judgment of most it would be most inappropriate for the Council of Bishops to control the handling and allocation of the many millions of dollars which Methodists contribute for many causes.

Finally in a book about primacy it is important to note

that American Methodism, including The United Methodist Church, has no primate. It has not had one since the death of John Wesley. There is no archbishop, no presiding bishop, no moderator or president. The Council of Bishops elects a president annually, but he is not regarded as the titular head of the denomination; in truth, most Methodists do not know who that president is. Closer to a permanent headship perhaps is the secretary of the Council of Bishops. This is a position of much political leverage, to be sure, but there is no statutory provision for it and certainly no relating of it to the concept of primacy.

Since the idea of primacy in Methodism is literally a vacuum, some have felt impelled to fill the empty space. They are impelled either by the traditional papal or patriarchal traditions in other churches, or else by the common sense notion that every organized body of people should have a single head. The one thought by some to be worthy of this place was the president of the World Methodist Council, a loose conglomerate of the Methodist churches. But this possibility was effectively ended when the World Methodist Council voted to have a presidium of eight instead of one.

There is little to suggest that the nearly two centuries of Methodist experience have engendered an attitude which is congenial to the notion of primacy. Yet we will examine the possibility of a more favorable attitude subsequently.

Meanwhile another dimension of the question of authority merits attention. Administrative exercise is not the only form. There is also the *teaching office*. Does The United Methodist Church have one? Not really. As there is no Methodist papacy, so there is no *magisterium*. In respect to this double lack, Methodism is like most other Protestant denominations. Methodists are more likely to say, "I believe this or that," rather than, "The Church teaches this."

Does this mean that The United Methodist Church has no definite doctrines? No—but how definite are they? Before being approved for ordination as elder, a person must answer a set of questions including these: "Have you studied the doctrines of

The United Methodist Church? Are they in full harmony with the Holy Scriptures? Will you preach and maintain them?" The candidate is expected to say yes to each question. But what is the content or substance of that affirmation? Doctrine means teaching. *What* does the church teach? *How* does it teach?

In the main line of American Methodism there have been two loci of doctrinal authority other than the Holy Scriptures themselves. These were formally adopted by The Methodist Episcopal Church in 1808 and still obtain. The first is the Twenty-five Articles of Religion, being John Wesley's own adaptation of the Thirty-nine Articles of the Church of England. The second is the work of Wesley himself: his *Forty-four Sermons* and his *Notes on the New Testament*. In these documents are found the formulations and informal interpretations of Wesley's evangelical catholicism and broad Anglicanism, expressed mainly in homily and exhortation, but often apologetic and polemical as well. For several generations, ordinands have been able to respond with an unabashed "yes" to the questions about doctrines, being firm in their knowledge that their examiners have been just as careless as they have been about reading the historic standards! This is said factually, not cynically. It is a fact that for many decades these "standards" have not been used to measure or test the faith of Methodists. (See the candid and constructive discussion of this problem in *The Discipline*, Part II.)

Several forces have been at work in bringing about a reform of this doctrinal carelessness. One is the ecumenical encounter; to meet its challenges many Methodist theologians have had to rediscover their roots and sources of identity. Related to this, secondly, is the recovery of the theology of John Wesley, with his distinctive teaching on the meaning of divine grace as well as his sacramental sensitivity and churchmanship. The third factor is the demand of the "modern mind" for theological clarity. The fourth is the example of the Second Vatican Council, which showed how a great and cumbersome gathering of bishops and theologians could enable the pope to exercise his magisterial role. Finally, the union of the former Methodist Church with the Evangelical United Brethren Church in 1968, forming the present denomination, provided the fitting occasion for a careful review by a Theological Study Commission on Doctrine and Doctrinal Standards. It is both astonishing and dismaying to observe that 160 years had passed since the adoption of the Wesleyan standards of doctrine, during which time the main denomination of American Methodism had felt no need for a formal theological commission.

One man deserves the greatest credit for making these Methodists see the value, or even necessity, of something like a *magisterium*. He is Professor Albert C. Outler, the foremost theological interpreter of John Wesley and a widely respected ecumenical scholar. His role as a Protestant observer at Vatican II was notable. And he did more than any other American theologian to bring many Protestants to a recognition of the indispensability of tradition in the common history of Christianity. His influence has opened the minds of many Methodists to a consideration of such a question as the primacy.

The Study Commission chaired by Outler did not produce a new doctrinal confession, creed or catechism. That was not its intention. But its report showed how present-day Methodists, sharing a sense of corporate ecclesial responsibility for explicating the truth of the Gospel, can arrive at teachable and preachable conclusions on perennial issues of faith. The mode or guideline for this is the fourfold method implicit in John Wesley's theology: starting with the witness of authoritative Holy Scripture, examining its meaning in the light of tradition, testing it in personal experience, and subjecting its conceptual formulation to reason. The report was adopted by a nearly unanimous vote of General Conference in 1972. Its salutary effect upon Methodist teaching remains to be seen.

We may note in summary that while it is impossible to state true generalizations for all Methodists, certain characteristics predominate which are pertinent to the ecumenical discussion of authority and primacy.

First, Methodists are long accustomed to the exercise of churchly authority by their conferences and bishops.

Second, the source of such authority, whether of God or of human will, has seldom been explored or defined.

Third, the ecumenical challenge and experience have stimulated a healthy new concern for the integrity of doctrine and the focusing of *consensus fidelium*, or the mind of the church.

II

AN APPRAISAL OF ACTUAL AND POTENTIAL
METHODIST ATTITUDES TOWARD PAPAL PRIMACY

The most fruitful theological conversations with Roman Catholics in recent years have been enjoyed by Anglicans, Lutherans and Calvinist-Reformed. Why have the Catholic-Methodist discussions been less intense and less productive? One reason among others stands out. It is the historical fact that Methodism never broke with Rome, because it had never been attached to Rome. The schism was once removed with Anglicanism coming in between. Churches of the other three kinds since the sixteenth century have always to some extent defined themselves over against Roman Catholicism. Thus recent ecumenical impulses have stimulated thoughts of the possibilities of rapprochement between Rome on the one hand and the symbolic cities of Canterbury, Wittenberg and Geneva on the other. Methodist attitudes toward the Catholic Church are neither informed by ancestral memories of disruption and controversy nor inspired by bright hopes of reconciliation.

John Wesley's irenicism as expressed in his "Letter to a Roman Catholic" was real enough, but its import for today has perhaps been inflated.[5] In the letter he avoided discussion of dogmatic or hierarchical issues and emphasized the unitive power of evangelical faith and the inspiring love of Christ. However, in sermons and writings Wesley also made good use of contemporary invective. He referred to the Catholic countries of Europe as "those lands which are overspread with Romish darkness."[6] He preached a great sermon on the "Catholic Spirit" in which he advocated much diversity within the unity of faith. But he also preached against "popery" and the Catholics' abuse of the Gospel as "the Romish delusion." He also went along with the very polemical phrases of the Thirty-nine Articles, which were transmitted to the American Methodist patrimony. Although Wesley has emerged today as a significant Christian personality, congenial to Catholic spirituality and classic doctrinal tradition, he hardly influences modern Methodists in their views of Catholicism.

From 1784 until 1958 most Methodists in America were as ignorant and distrustful of the Catholic Church as they were detached and alienated from it. Catholic attitudes toward Methodism were much the same. The coming of Pope John XXIII "in the fullness of time" caused a sudden shift of perspective, of course. A measure of that change of heart was the formal communication which the General Conference of 1970 felt disposed to send to Pope Paul VI. It was a declaration of intent by which Methodists annulled the anti-Catholic biases of the Twenty-five Articles. Since the Constitution restricts the General Conference from altering these old articles, the best which could be said was that the prejudicial phrases no longer expressed Methodist sentiments. The pope received this graciously. Such was a good fruit of the Second Vatican Council.

The constitutions and decrees of that council were not addressed to such churches as the United Methodist, so no formal response to Rome could be expected. The conciliar documents were widely read and systematically studied by many Methodists, however. In particular, *Lumen gentium*, the Constitution on the Church, has dramatized both the nearness and the distance.

Methodists who are serious about biblical theology as a guide for present faith, and who have not been seduced by the lures of ultra-liberal reductionism, welcome certain portions of this document with the "enthusiasm" which allegedly is the mark of their faith. The chapters on the mystery of the church, on the people of God, on the laity, and on the call to holiness are all most congenial to the Methodist understanding of the church and the Christian life. It does not matter that the chapter on the laity seems unduly tentative and hesitant about the full participation of lay people in the affairs and decisions of the church, for a great stride has been taken away from the traditional Roman clericalism. Nor must Methodists reject the chapter on holiness because it inevitably holds up the ideal of sacerdotal and religious celibacy; in the main it describes the way of sanctified living which coincides with the Wesleyan ideal.[7]

It is Chapter III of *Lumen gentium* which reminds even the most ecumenically committed Methodist that the distance to Rome is very long, with major obstacles blocking the access. None would have supposed that the Council fathers of 1965 would have ignored, much less repealed, the dogmatic constitution of 1870 on the primacy and infallibility of the bishop of Rome. They declared: "And all this teaching about the institution, the perpetuity, the force and reason for the sacred primacy of the Roman pontiff and of his infallible teaching authority, this sacred Synod again proposes to be firmly believed by all the faithful."[8]

If the primacy and infallibility of the pontiff are required *de fide* of Catholics, including the divinely ordained continuity of St. Peter's commission through the succession of popes, so also must the nature of episcopacy be believed. *Lumen gentium* continues after a delay of ninety-five years the agenda of the First Vatican Council. It assumes the full legitimacy of the traditional theory: that Jesus Christ "formed after the manner of a college or fixed group" the twelve disciples, entrusted and inspired them for the mission of salvation which "will last until the end of the world," and thus made it incumbent upon them "to appoint successors in this hierarchically structured society" which is the Catholic Church. "Therefore, this sacred Synod teaches that by divine institution bishops have succeeded to the place of the apostles as shepherds of the Church, and that he who hears them, hears Christ, while he who rejects them, rejects Christ and him who sent Christ."[9]

These familiar reassertions about the apostolic succession of bishops, and of the bishop of Rome in particular, are manifestly integral to Roman Catholic doctrine. Even though Catholic biblical scholars and theologians have felt free, as never before, to conclude that the New Testament does not give unchallenged support for this theory, it is unlikely that any serious modification of it will be accepted as official teaching.

Equally evident is the sheer unlikelihood that Methodists will be persuaded to acknowledge the veracity of Roman claims for pope and episcopacy. As has been shown above, the Methodist episcopacy may exhibit some external similarities to that of Catholicism, and some Methodist bishops may even feel the attraction of a theory or doctrine of succession. Indeed, this has become a live option in some of the church union discussions with Anglicans. But there is nothing within the theological scope of Methodist belief which can be correlated, much less identified, with the Catholic position.

Does this negation mean that nothing more can be thought or said about a drawing together of Methodism and Catholicism on the matter of hierarchy and primacy? Not at all. This may have seemed to be the absolute impasse before 1965. It is not so today. The ecumenical mood of mutual acceptance as real Christians and real churches makes it at least plausible to think thoughts which until recently were unthinkable. As for Methodists, it is no doubt true that only a very small proportion of them are giving thought to the unthinkable, so what follows may not be regarded as representative of the thought and attitude of other than a tiny minority. Yet, in the long-range historical continuum of the church and in view of the necessity of unity for the Christian faith and church, it may prove to be the truly creative minority.

The premises regarding primacy, as agreeable to Methodists, are these:

1. *Authority in the church is acknowledged only as an aid to mission.* The keynote was sounded by the risen Lord in the so-called Great Commission (Matthew 28:19): "All authority is given unto (Christ) in heaven and on earth. . . . Go, therefore, and make disciples. . . ."

Given the fallenness of human nature, it is unlikely that anyone can exercise authority over another person in a purely equitable, just, altruistic and loving way. The authority of Jesus Christ may well be of that quality, but when it devolves upon human beings it suffers corruption and abuse. This does not mean that all persons want to abuse the authority they wield. It just happens that they do. In the candid observations of history, this imperfection distorts papal authority as readily as that of a Methodist bishop or district superintendent. John Wesley was not exempt from it, nor were the best of popes.

It is unreal and romantic to pretend that the church as a diverse and cumbersome community of men and women does not need to have certain appointed or recognized leaders to exercise authority in various ways. But to what end? Ultimately to serve the end of advancing the mission of Christ for human salvation. The Catholic scholar, John L. McKenzie, is surely right in stating this principle categorically: "The nature of authority in the Church and the use of authority are determined by the mission of the Church, which is to proclaim the Gospel. Authority is empowered to act within the terms of this mission and within no other terms."[10]

In fairness to John Wesley, it can be presumed that in his self-awareness as a virtually monarchical leader of the movement he was guided by this missional principle. Everything, including the church, was secondary in importance to the saving of souls, and everything about the church was ancillary to that purpose. In fairness to history, however, it must be admitted that many Methodist leaders, while cognizant of this principle, have disregarded it.

Is it possible within the confines of human fallibility for some Christian person occupying the place of primacy among all Christians of the world to let his use of this awesome authority be wholly determined by the human needs of food, work, liberty, health, moral integrity and divine salvation? No Methodist will be persuaded that God intends the first place of authority in his church to be just an impersonal office. But one might be convinced of the legitimacy and desirability of a place of worldwide primacy if the holders of it were constantly recognized by their acts—*Acta Apostolicae Sedis!*—as personifications and leaders of the wide and diverse scope of Christ's mission. And if Methodists were inclined to apply the same criterion to their own bishops and other leaders, so much the better for all concerned.

Now, this idea needs to be examined critically. It is obviously impossible to keep legitimating the place of primacy every few years by the acts of each incumbent. Further, his acts could not be judged until he had already been in office for a time. So it would seem logical to fall back, after all, on belief in the validity of the office regardless of the behavior of its holder. But there may be a way out of this vicious circle. It would be the way of modifying two things. First, the ecclesiastical environment in which the primate lives and operates could be changed, eliminating as much as possible the temptations and obligations which distract him from the primal task of leading the Christian mission in the world. Second, the expectations which church members have of this exalted ministry could be altered, allowing him to be truly *servus servorum Dei* rather than *dominus* or *pontifex*. There is a swelling stream of writing about the papacy which urges such change and reform in a radical manner and with minimal delay. The examples of both John XXIII and Paul VI point already to such a possibility: the former exuding the personal love and joy of Christ, the latter flying to four continents outside Europe to dramatize the universality of the Christian faith.

2. *The false connotation of the title, vicar of Christ, must be corrected, if indeed it is to be retained at all.* A popular idea conflicts with a biblical insight. If the pope is regarded as the

head of the church, how can it be accepted that Jesus Christ is the sole head of his body, the church? Either there are two heads, which is grotesque to consider; or else the two are really one. Catholic piety has been disposed to support the latter explanation. The pope is thus the only vicar, or fully empowered representative, of the risen and ascended Christ. So he is designated in *Lumen gentium*: "The vicar of Christ and the visible head of the whole Church."[11]

Like most Christians, Methodists have no difficulty in believing that the risen Christ lives now in his people. It is a fundamental and persistent teaching of St. Paul and indispensable to Christian faith that Christ lives in us and we in him. This is the work of the Holy Spirit, the Comforter or Advocate, whom the ascended Christ gave in order to effect personal union with himself. Through the Spirit, as Martin Luther perceived the New Testament witness, the true vicar of Christ is every faithful person who is united with Christ. Hence, the priesthood of all believers is authenticated by the eternal priesthood of Christ in the heavenly places.

Catholics have been prone for many generations to repeat the assertion made in 1439 by the Council of Florence, an event which was intended to unite the Greek Orthodox and Roman Catholic Churches. The assertion was: "The Roman pontiff himself is the successor of Peter, prince of the apostles . . . the true vicar of Christ, head of the whole Church, father and teacher of all Christians."[12] (No wonder the Orthodox in Greece and Byzantium rejected this compromise made by their delegates!) But this fifteenth-century statement, repeated verbatim in 1870, was a creation of the Western tradition. When first used in the third century, the title of vicar applied mainly to the bishops, while the bishop of Rome was likely to be called the vicar of Peter.[13] *Lumen gentium* also recognizes the more ancient designation when it says that the bishops are vicars of Christ in their own right, not vicars of the Roman pontiff.[14]

Methodists would resist the belief that Christ works in his church by designating a few people to be, in effect, his *alter ego* or even his plenipotentiary. They would never admit this with respect to their own bishops nor to bishops of other churches, unless indeed they accepted the whole doctrine of apostolic succession as interpreted by the Second Vatican Council. Much greater would be the difficulty in espousing the belief in one man only as the true vicar of Christ on earth. The possibility of gaining assent to an ecumenical primacy thus hinges in part on the disposition of Catholics to modify this usage.

3. *Primacy of and for the church depends upon the real exercise of collegiality.* We have seen how the instrument of the conference from local to national levels is the integral hallmark of Methodist polity. Extended to the global dimension, this would imply the need for a world conference, representative of all different constituents. And somehow within that ecumenical convocation the primate would find his place of collegial relationship.

One of the most welcome developments in contemporary Catholic thought and practice is the conception and growing practice of collegiality. This marks a repudiation of that corrupt and expendable idea that the priest is the autocrat of his parish, the bishop of his diocese, and the pope of the whole church. By affirming co-responsibility for the life and mission of the church, Catholics are effecting remarkable changes for the better. This does not mean simply that Catholics are becoming more like Methodists. In one way, indeed, they are surpassing Methodists in their quest for genuine collegiality: that is, they are thinking through the theological meaning of collegiality and subsidiarity, rather than following a conventional secular model of democratic organization, such as the Methodist conferences tend sometimes to be. The proper question is not "How can church members conduct their business in a parliamentary manner so as to reach majority decision?" but rather "How is the will of Christ appropriated and effectuated in his body, the church?"

If *Lumen gentium* marks a new stage in Catholic thinking by highlighting collegiality, it is also quite explicit in defining

what this means. And it is not what Methodists or other Protestants think it means. Collegiality is said to reside in the
whole college of bishops, where it pertains to teaching authority and pastoral rule. Yet this great body of bishops—hundreds
of them—is not capable of exercising its given power without
the consent of the Roman pontiff. The college of bishops can
act with full power over the church, but only together with the
pope and never without him. In practice since 1967, as we have
seen, this means that the pope seeks collegial counsel by con-
vening the synod of bishops, but he is not bound to accept their
counsel if he chooses otherwise. He is both a member of the
college of bishops and yet is above and apart from the others.

Must it be this way? No small number of Catholic theologians have been critical of Paul VI as well as of the Council for
not giving a greater measure of power to the synod of bishops.
Thus, for example, Wilhelm de Vries, S.J. urged that the pope
should be obliged to support any decision of the synod of bishops which was reached by a three-fourths majority.[15] This
would not make the pope a mere spokesman for the synod, but
it would require him to recognize in such a vote the authentic
consensus of the whole church, which if truly indefectible represents the divine will in this instance.

A typically Protestant view of papal primacy as conditioned by collegiality is that of Gérard Siegwalt of Strassbourg.
He sees the pope as president of the synod or council, which
rightly represents the whole church, but as president he is more
than the presiding officer: he is "a personalized ministry of
unity." This means that in his person he embodies the collegial
thinking of the church and also speaks authoritatively for it.[16]
The college must have a presiding head lest it be anarchical
and unable to speak in concert. And the head, or president,
must have a college lest he be simply an autocrat. So in theory,
at least, Protestants might look favorably upon the primacy. It
would then be a proper analogy to the relation of Peter to the
other apostles, rather than the ontological succession to their
respective offices. That this interpretation is possible for Cath-

olics seems to be suggested by the important but often overlooked "Prefatory Notes of Explanation" which was published
as an addendum to *Lumen gentium*. There is stated the following proposition: "The parallel between Peter and the other
apostles on the one hand, and the supreme pontiff and the bishops on the other, does not imply any transmission of the extraordinary power of the apostles to their successors, nor, as is
clear, any *equality* between the head and the members of the
college, but only a *proportionality* between the first relationship (Peter/apostles) and the second (pope/bishops)."[17]

4. *Primacy informed by the spirit of collegiality requires
as its corollary a broader practice of conciliarism.* This statement of a possible Methodist attitude toward primacy goes
beyond the question of proportionality between pope and bishops. By conciliarism, or conciliarity, would be meant a convocation much more inclusive and representative of the membership of the church than the present synod of bishops or even
the ecumenical council as defined by Roman Catholic standards. Take the Second Vatican Council as the most recent example. Certainly it differed radically from the Council of 1870
and all those which preceded it. Thanks to the warm heart and
open mind of John XXIII and the enlightened counsel he received from certain cardinals and theological advisers, this
council was an event of positive significance for all Christian
churches, and especially for those which were represented by
official observers. But was it an *ecumenical* council?

In Roman Catholic reckoning it was the Twenty-first Ecumenical Council. It conformed to the definition contained in
one of its own documents: "A council is never ecumenical
unless it is confirmed or at least accepted by the successor of
Peter. It is the prerogative of the Roman pontiff to convoke
these councils, to preside over them, and to confirm them."[18]

A most sympathetic and ecumenically-minded Russian
Orthodox observer, Protopresbyter Vitaly Borovoy, expressed
the mind and faith of his tradition when he said that Vatican II
was an excellent council for Roman Catholics, with much in-

terest for all, but it was not an ecumenical one.[19] Canonically considered, the Orthodox recognize only the first seven councils as truly ecumenical, and the eighth has not yet met.

Insofar as Protestants think of conciliarism, it is fair to say that Vatican II was deficient as an ecumenical event for two reasons. First, as the Orthodox point out, it was officially limited to Catholic delegates. And, second, since it was a council of prelates who had been appointed to their episcopal office in the first place by the Vatican, the broad membership of the church was present neither by delegation nor by representation.

Thus the literally ecumenical character of this recent council must be called into question. Since the council itself agreed that the Roman Catholic Church is not in itself the whole church, that the Church of Christ *subsists* in the Church of Rome, and that other Christian churches are truly to be called churches, it seems reasonable to judge that the council raised the same question of its own ecumenicity.

Vatican II did not resolve the very old dispute within the Catholic Church on the relation of council to pope. This was the great internal issue of the fifteenth century, of course, when popes and conciliar fathers fought for power in the Councils of Constance, Basel and Florence. After five centuries the question is still unsettled in the minds of many Catholics.[20] And certainly non-Catholics cannot be satisfied with the definition of *Lumen gentium* cited above, nor can they accept as legitimate the kind of intervention of Paul VI in revising the text of a report to his own satisfaction and without a due and proper vote of the whole body.

There is no common Protestant, nor even Methodist, mind on this matter, other than the negative observations just indicated. However, a theory is germinating in the World Council of Churches which in time might become an acceptable ecumenical concept of conciliarity. Rather modestly it was proposed by the report of the Fourth Assembly at Uppsala, Sweden, 1968 that the churches are moving toward the time of "a genuinely universal council." The character of such a coun-

cil will require much time to define, and the holding of it will
depend upon the pace of the movement for Christian unity.[21]
The idea implies for Protestants at least three rejections. It
rejects the Orthodox doctrine that only a pan-Orthodox pro-
synod could convoke such a council, since there is no longer a
Byzantine emperor to do so. It also disagrees with the Roman
teaching just described. And it definitely does not mean that
the World Council of Churches is, or can be, a genuinely universal council, but only at best its precursor. So is it all an impossible dream? We do not know. It may be that the ecumenical momentum in Western Christianity, both Catholic and
Protestant, will carry these churches toward a common council
with a single president or primate. But would it then be only
Western, since the Eastern doctrine on councils seems to be immutable and immovable?

In any case, and remote as the time of realization may be,
the primacy will have to be one which is representative of, and
subordinate to, the universal council.

5. *The "Petrine office" can have contemporary support
by non-Catholics if it signifies "first among equals."* It is a
strange fact that many Protestants in this era of ecumenism
have had to overcome an inbred disrespect for St. Peter simply
because his name was associated with the papacy—and the
papacy was obviously bad! Thus Peter's role in the Gospels
was minimized, the epistles ascribed to him were little read,
and he was more often the gatekeeper in a tiresome joke about
heaven than the foremost of the disciples, apostles and martyrs.
If the writing of Oscar Cullmann served to rehabilitate the person of Peter in the estimation of Protestant theologians, it has
been the bi-lateral conversations between Lutherans and
Roman Catholics which have helped Protestants appreciate
Peter's importance for the contemporary church.[22] Even
though few Protestants are honestly able to affirm the theory
and the doctrine of direct papal succession from the prince of
apostles, with all that "the power of keys" suggests, two things
are becoming clearer and more acceptable. One is that Peter

did indeed enjoy a special relationship to Jesus and occupy a unique place among the disciples; thus the disputed words of Matthew 16:18-19 cannot be explained away as the later insertions of Catholic belief. The second is that the church today, as always, needs someone to exercise what the Lutheran-Roman Catholic common statement calls the "Petrine function." These admissions do not constitute adequate grounds for embracing the whole Catholic teaching, to be sure, but they have opened the way for Lutherans at least to have an enhanced appreciation for the concept of primacy.

The Orthodox view of papacy and the perspective of many Anglicans have not required a restudy of the Petrine tradition in order to give a positive appraisal of a qualified or modified primacy. In relation to the other patriarchs and presiding archbishops of the autocephalous churches, the ecumenical patriarch of Constantinople enjoys a spiritual primacy. The archbishop of Canterbury has no canonical authority over other churches of the Anglican Communion, but there is never a doubt as to his priority among them. Both Patriarch Athenagoras I before his death and Archbishop A. Michael Ramsey before his retirement indicated their willingness to look upon the bishop of Rome as patriarch of the West (which is one of his proper titles) and, if certain conditions were fulfilled, *primus inter pares*.

It would be fatuous to suggest that Methodists by and large have a comparable view of the primacy or of the Petrine function. Methodists have not engaged the issue, as have Lutherans with their theological zest and thoroughness. Nor do Methodists have a tradition which in any sense resembles the Orthodox and the Anglican primacies. And it is most doubtful that a distinctively Methodist position is going to be developed. More plausible and useful will be an effort on the part of Methodists to appropriate the scholarly work done by the Lutheran and Catholic scholars, to reflect upon the advantages for Christianity as a whole to have a collegial head with spiritual rather than juridical primacy, and then to hope for such

self-initiated changes in Catholic thinking as will make the
first-among-equals position acceptable to all. These changes,
we suggest, would need to be along the lines already indicated
in the preceding sections of this essay. They would be for the
peace and. unity and mission of the whole church. For as Father de Vries spoke the simple truth: "Only a primacy which is
understood as service and whose exercise excludes every suspicion of arbitrariness has the possibility of being accepted by
other Christians and is enabled to be, instead of an impediment
to unity, its actual guarantee."[23]

NOTES

1. *The Book of Discipline of the United Methodist Church*, Nashville,
1972, p. 143.
2. Quoted by Gerald F. Moede in an excellent discussion of Wesley's
episcopal-style of administration: *The Office of Bishop in Methodism*,
Zurich: Gotthelf Verlag, 1964, pp. 15-18.
3. *Ibid.*
4. "We can say that, in the sense and to the extent that the whole
Church is completely present in the local Church, the Church's powers of jurisdiction and order are completely present in the local bishop": Karl
Rahner, *Studies in Modern Theology*, Freiburg: Herder, 1965, p. 321.
5. The Irish ecumenist, Michael Hurley, S.J., has reminded Methodists
of this element in their own heritage by editing John Wesley's *Letter to a
Roman Catholic*, New York: Abingdon, 1968.
6. Quoted by Albert C. Outler, *John Wesley*, New York: Oxford University Press, 1964, p. 225.
7. The Roman Catholic-United Methodist dialogue in America has
resulted in a common statement on spirituality and holiness in the ministry,
to be issued in 1976.
8. *Lumen gentium*, III:18.
9. *Lumen gentium*, III:20.
10. John L. McKenzie, *Authority in the Church*, New York: Doubleday
(Image Book), 1971, p. 76.
11. *Lumen gentium*, III:18.
12. Denziger, *Enchiridion Symbolorum*, ed. A. Schonmetzer, 33rd edition, Rome, 1965; para. 1307, 332. Quoted and discussed by Francis Oakley,
Council over Pope? New York: Herder, 1969, pp. 84ff.
13. Msgr. Philips, *L'Eglise et son Mystère au deuxieme Concile du Vatican*, Paris: Desclée, 1967, Tome I, p. 228.
14. *Lumen gentium*, III:27.

15. At the Jesuits' International Conference on Ecumenism, Dublin, 1971.

16. "Authority in the Church" in *The Gospel and the Ambiguity of the Church*, edited by Vilmos Vajta, Philadelphia: Fortress, 1974, p. 206.

17. *The Documents of Vatican II*, edited by Walter M. Abbott, New York: Herder, 1966, p. 99.

18. *Lumen gentium*, III:22.

19. In a Faith and Order consultation held in Rome, 1968.

20. Among many references see especially Hans Küng, *Structures of the Church*, New York: Nelson, 1964; Francis Oakley, *Council over Pope?* New York: Herder, 1969.

21. See W. B. Blakemore, "The Potentiality of Conciliarity: Communion, Conscience, Council," in *No Man Is Alien*, edited by J. Robert Nelson, Leiden: Brill, 1971, pp. 225-244.

22. This is reflected in Dr. Burgess' article in this same volume.

23. Wilhelm de Vries, S.J., "Limits of Papal Primacy," paper delivered at Dublin, 1971.

Anglicans and the Papacy

J. Robert Wright

This must begin with some words about Episcopalians and their sense of history as members of the worldwide Anglican Communion of Churches. An historical survey of any major question under debate, such as the papacy, is of the highest importance for Anglicans, because it is from a concept of historical continuity that Anglicanism gets much of its own identity. For Anglicans, the sense of authority, of *magisterium*, is found less in the latest decrees of some centralized office than in a study of historical development from which certain trends emerge that can then be assessed in view of a variety of possible interpretations. To such a study, then, we first turn. Next will follow my own estimates, proceeding from the historical evidence, of the sort of papacy that would *not* be acceptable to Anglicans today and then the sort that *might* be. Finally I shall sketch out what I believe the next steps may be, both in the way of official agreements and also as regards practical matters.

Historical Survey

Forged in the furnace of Reformation controversy, the Henrician anti-papal legislation[1] pushed the medieval statutes of *Provisors* and *Praemunire* to their extremes and forced the practical implementation of royal claims that since the four-

176

teenth century for the most part had been theories held in a careful balance of working compromise between king and pope. As the crown began to assume theoretical as well as actual control over the English Church in the 1530's, especially in the areas of ecclesiastical courts, episcopal appointments, and church taxation, the papacy came to be viewed as the major enemy of the English Church in a way that had not been so before.[2] Whether or not the English Church in the Middle Ages enjoyed a degree of independence from papal authority greater than that of other national provinces (and this is still a subject of scholarly dispute),[3] it is certainly clear that the relative positions of crown and pope in the nation's past history were rewritten at this time to make it seem so.[4] Especially in the works of such mid-sixteenth-century chroniclers as William Tyndale, John Bale, and John Foxe, the story of the English Church throughout the Middle Ages was worked over and made to seem the history of a vast and sustained international conspiracy on the part of antichrist as represented by the popes and their minions, particularly the archbishops of Canterbury, to elevate clerical authority and reduce the English kings to submission.[5] In fact there was a continuity of much traditional catholic faith and practice, and in a paper of this brevity there is no room to assess either the manifold factors causing the English Reformation or the extent to which they were justified, but for present purposes we may conclude by observing that the papal connection was indeed broken and that the pope of Rome bore the major brunt of the polemic.[6] The medieval English tradition was in this way made to seem much more anti-papal than had in fact been the case.

Perhaps not surprising in view of an already incipient Anglican emphasis upon the principle of *lex orandi lex credendi*, this anti-papal polemic found its way into some of the earliest liturgical expressions authorized by the English reformers,[7] and so it is that in the first English Litany (1544) we find the deprecation clause "From the tyranny of the Bysshop of Rome and al hys detestable enormities . . . Good Lord, deliver us."

Incorporated into the first and second English prayer books, this clause was not discarded until the third (Elizabethan) book of 1559.[8]

Doctrinal formularies also gave expression to this Anglican position now, and the denial of papal claims in Article 36 of the Forty-two Articles of 1553 came to take its final place in the Church of England's Thirty-nine Articles of 1563/71 with the following words of Article 37 on Civil Magistrates: "The Bishop of Rome hath no jurisdiction in this Realm of England."[9] The temporal claims of the Roman see may have been as much or more the object of this denial as any implicit spiritual supervision, and it is significant that this clause about papal jurisdiction was omitted altogether and the rest of this article entirely rewritten when the English Articles were adapted for the Episcopal Church in America by its General Convention of 1801.

Classical Anglican apologetic soon found its first chief spokesman in the bishop of Salisbury, John Jewel, who wrote his *Apology of the Church of England* in 1562. The following passage[10] from it is worth quoting for its importance as an influential early example of the Anglican method whereby the Henrician political severance of the papal connection came to be given theological justification on grounds of a patristic golden age:

Tell us, I pray you, good Holy Father, seeing ye do crack so much of all antiquity and boast yourself that all men are bound to you alone, which of all the fathers have at any time called you by the name of the highest prelate, the universal bishop or head of the church? Which of them ever said that both the swords were committed to you? Which of them ever said that you have authority and right to call councils? Which of them ever said that the whole world is your diocese? Which of them, that all bishops have received of your fullness? Which of them, that all power is given to you as well in heaven as in earth? Which of them, that neither kings, nor the whole clergy, nor yet all people together, are able to be judges over you? Which of them, that kings and emperors by Christ's commandment and will do receive authority at your hand? Which of them, that more ample authority is given to you than to the residue of the patriarchs? Which of them, that you are the Lord God? Or that you are not a mere natural man but a certain substance made and grown together of God and man? Which of them, that you are the only headspring of all law? Which of them, that you have power over purgatories? Which of them, that you are able to command the angels of God as you list yourself? Which of them that ever said that you are Lord of lords and the King of kings? We can also go further with you in like sort. What one amongst the whole number of the old bishops and fathers ever taught you either to say private Mass while the people stared on or to lift up the sacrament over your head (in which point consisteth now all your religion); or else to mangle Christ's sacraments and to bereave the people of the one part, contrary to Christ's institution and plain expressed words? But, that we may once come to an end, what one is there of all the fathers which hath taught you to distribute Christ's blood and the holy martyr's merits, and to sell openly as merchandises your pardons and all the rooms and lodgings of purgatory? These men are wont to speak much of a certain secret doctrine of theirs and manifold and sundry readings. Then let them bring forth somewhat now, if they can, that it may appear they have at least read or do know somewhat. They have often stoutly noised in all corners where they went how all the parts of their religion be very old and have been approved not only by the multitude but also by the consent and continual observation of all nations and times. Let them therefore once in their life show this their antiquity. Let them make appear at eye that the things whereof they make such ado have taken so long and large increase. Let them declare

that all Christian nations have agreed by consent to this
their religion. . . . They have not, good Lord, they have
not (I say) those things which they boast they have: they
have not that antiquity, they have not that universality,
they have not that consent of all places nor of all times.

Jewel, to be sure, did not deny that in the ancient church the
bishop of Rome had "an estimation, and a credit, and a prerogative before others," indeed "the first place" among the
four ancient patriarchs, but Jewel insisted that he had held this
position only by reason of various historical accidents: the antiquity of the Roman see, the glory of its martyrs, the imperial
position of Rome itself, and the purity of the Christian religion
that had been preserved there—a purity that Rome had long
since lost. With that purity now gone, Rome held no prerogative by any sort of divine right.[11]

This strongly negative Anglican view of the papacy can be
traced in still other sources of the time, not the least of which is
the inaugural lecture of the future archbishop of Canterbury,
John Whitgift, given upon his becoming Lady Margaret Professor of Divinity at Cambridge University in 1563 on the popular theme "The pope is antichrist."[12] This same character-
ization of the pope, already sounded in the invectives of
Tyndale, Bale, and Foxe, is also present in the works of Jewel
himself, of Richard Hooker, of James Ussher, and of King
James I.[13]

Cut off in this rather vitriolic way from any further consideration of the papal obedience, the Anglican theological tradition began to have its own development now, both catholic
and reformed, without direct reference to the mainstream of
Roman Catholic life and thought. A thorough and careful history of Anglican attitudes toward the papacy from the Reformation to the present, yet to be written and much to be desired,[14] would—I believe—reveal many interesting shifts as well
as a persistent evolution. King James I may well have set the
first stage for a more realistic reassessment of the Henrician

and Elizabethan theologians' views in his *Premonition to All
. . . Monarchs* (1609):

> Patriarchs I know were in the time of the Primitive
> Church, and I likewise reverence that institution for order
> sake; and amongst them was a contention for the first
> place. And for myself (if that were yet the question) I
> would with all my heart give my consent that the Bishop
> of Rome should have the first seat; I being a Western
> King would go with the Patriarch of the West. And for his
> temporal principality over the Signory of Rome, I do not
> quarrel it either. Let him in God His Name be *Primus
> Episcopus inter omnes Episcopos*, and *Princeps Epis-
> coporum*, so it be no otherwise but as Peter was *Princeps
> Apostolorum*. But as I well allow of the hierarchy of the
> Church for distinction of orders (for so I understand it), so
> I utterly deny that there is an earthly Monarch thereof,
> whose word must be a law, and who cannot err in his sen-
> tence, by an Infallibility of Spirit.[15]

We may note that the seventeenth-century divines, although
some are much exercised over the problem of infallibility as
they see it, on the whole strike a more balanced and at times
moderate note.[16] Many of them, such as the first King James,
Archbishop John Bramhall of Armagh, and others, readily acknowledge a primacy in Rome and that the pope should be
first among all bishops.[17] Both Bishop John Cosin of Durham
and King James were willing to call him "Patriarch of the
West."[18] Bramhall and Archbishop William Laud could accord
him a "primacy of order, of place, of pre-eminence," but not of
power.[19] Bramhall and Isaac Barrow both appeal to Cyprian's
De Unitate in support of such views.[20] Even the invectives
against infallibility penned by such men as William Chillingworth,[21] Jeremy Taylor,[22] Henry Dodwell,[23] and George
Hicks[24] are written with little reference to the actual Roman
experience of the post-Tridentine papacy, and it is such works

as these that set the tone for an Anglican "case" against the doctrine of infallibility long before it was defined at the First Vatican Council of 1870.

The purpose of the present essay being a contrast rather than an exhaustive study, we shall now move past the following centuries, omitting consideration except by title of the papal interests of the Oxford Movement reformers, up to the twentieth century. Here we may see a remarkable contrast to the invectives of former ages, and indeed not a few opinions that can at least be described as irenic. First we may cite a theologian participating in the Malines Conversations of 1921-1925 who, it is said, "did not include Anglo-Catholicism among his crimes": J. Armitage Robinson, the Dean of Wells, was prepared to accord the Roman see "a general superintendence, a care for the well-being of the churches as a whole," and wished for "much more than a simple primacy of honour" for the pope.[25]

Other Anglican church historians had similar views. B. J. Kidd, Warden of Keble and another Malines theologian, wrote in 1936 of the Roman primacy: "It was a primacy of leadership, more than a primacy of honour though less than a primacy of jurisdiction, and the bishop of Rome as occupant of the first apostolic see in Christendom derives from St. Peter and St. Paul, the twin founders in the sense of organizers of the church in Rome, that pre-eminence which has been accorded to him everywhere, always and by all and is still generally recognized as his." H. E. Symmonds, in his study of early relations between the papacy and the episcopate (1939), concluded, "The episcopate was one in essence and ideal. But this unity had its centre in the apostolic see of Rome. This centre . . . is not indeed of such necessity that all cut off from it are by that fact cut off from membership within the Church of Christ. Yet in the eyes of all it was the see to which all Christians looked." And Dr. T. G. Jalland of Exeter in his Bampton Lectures (1944) observed, "The Roman see was recognized by other churches as possessing from early times, if not from the beginning, an undoubted primacy in the sphere of doctrine, at least in the sense of a right to be heard in preference to others. . . . The right of the papacy to act as supreme judge in matters of discipline, if not traceable so far back as the doctrinal primacy, is at least contemporary in respect of its development with the evolution of episcopal jurisdiction."

The former archbishop of Canterbury, Dr. Michael Ramsey, in his first major theological work (*The Gospel and the Catholic Church*, 1936), struck a note which, perhaps ahead of its day in the climate of the 1930's, nevertheless has a curiously contemporary ring to one who studies the evaluations of the papacy being made in our own time:

> It was stated in Chapter V that a Papacy which acted as an organ of the Church's general consciousness and authority in doctrine, and which focused the unity of the one Episcopate might claim to fulfill the tests of true development. And it was further stated in Chapter XI that at certain times in history the Papacy conspicuously failed to do this and has thereby been the means of perverting the real meaning of Catholicism. But this historical fact cannot justify a wholesale refusal to consider the Petrine claims. Other organs in the one Body have had their times of failure and of self-aggrandisement, and we do not therefore conclude that they must be discarded. Hence it seems possible that in the reunited Church of the future there may be a special place for a *"primus-inter-pares"* as an organ of unity and authority. Peter will be needed as well as Paul and Apollos, and like them he will be chastened and repentant.[26]

Finally, the document which is perhaps the nearest thing to a comprehensive and in some way quasi-official statement of Anglican doctrine, the report of the commission appointed by the archbishops of Canterbury and York entitled *Doctrine in the Church of England* (1938), constructed a very cautious balance in its own conclusions which probably represent, if not the

clear hard thinking of some one person like Ramsey, at least
an honest evaluation of the total spectrum of Anglican thinking
on the papacy at this time:[27]

> We are united in holding that the Church of England was
> right to take the stand which it took in the sixteenth centu-
> ry and is still bound to resist the claims of the contem-
> porary Papacy. The account which we have already given
> of the nature of spiritual and doctrinal authority supplies
> in large measure the ground of our conviction on this
> point. With regard to the Church of the future, some of us
> look forward to a reunion of Christendom having its
> centre in a Primacy such as might be found in a Papacy
> which had renounced certain of its present claims; some,
> on the other hand, look forward to union by a more feder-
> al type of constitution which would have no need for such
> a Primacy.

By the eve of the Second Vatican Council, then, even in
the absence of an exhaustive historical survey, I think we can
say that the Anglican view of the papacy had evolved from the
consciously "anti-papal" polemic of the sixteenth century to an
attitude which in the mid-twentieth century can at least be
called "non-papal" by contrast.

And in more recent times since Vatican II, there are indications that this "non-papal" stance has for at least some
Anglicans proceeded to an expressed interest in exploring the
possibilities that some form of actual papal leadership may
offer to the one church of the future. The senior Anglican
delegate-observer at Vatican II, Bishop Moorman of Ripon,
has made the following comments (1966 and 1967):[28]

> Whether we like it or not, things can never be the same
> again (*since the Second Vatican Council*). In the ecumeni-
> cal world Rome has, to some extent, taken the initiative,
> and the question now being asked is: "What is the rest of
> Christendom going to do about it? How does this apply to

the Anglican Communion?" The Anglican Communion began as a "national" Church—the Church of the English people—and, to some extent, it still preserves that characteristic, although it has spread all over the world. Many would like to continue as such; but the days of "national Churches" are over, and the Anglican Communion will probably have to join up sooner or later with one or other of the main "families" or groups of Christians. There are three such "families"—Roman, Orthodox, and Reformed. Here it is interesting to note that, roughly speaking, of every ten people in the world, six are non-Christian, two are Roman Catholic, one is Orthodox, and one Reformed (that is, Lutheran, Anglican, Calvinist, Methodist, Baptist, etc.). With which of these three "families" should the Anglican Communion eventually find its home? . . . To a great many Anglicans any idea of union with Rome seems quite out of the question. We have had so many years of bitterness, misunderstanding and fear that the obstacles would seem insuperable. But the Vatican Council has made a big difference. Rome is now very anxious to enter into dialogue and discussions with Anglicans, realizing that, behind our differences, we have much in common. . . . The problem as I see it has nothing to do with subjection or submission. The ultimate position of the Pope in relation to other bishops would depend upon Christian unity, and what sort of Church emerged out of the prayers and labours of Christian people. There is no question here of the Roman Catholic Church absorbing all other Christian Churches, but of the whole Christian world trying to rediscover and restore the one Church which Christ founded and which in the course of time has become split up through man's sin and folly.

In several recent sermons delivered on the west coast, moreover, Bishop Kilmer Myers of California had strong words to say on the same subject:[29]

What I therefore wish to say—for your further reflection
—is that we Anglican and Protestant Christians ought to
re-examine our relationship to the Holy See as the chief
spokesman for the Christian community in the world. In
doing this I am not suggesting that in any sense we abject-
ly crawl to the feet of the Pope to ask his forgiveness and
acceptance. The Second Vatican Council and indeed Pope
Paul have pointed to the division of blame among all
Christian communities for the present disunity of the
Church. The Roman Catholic Church clearly is accepting
its own share of the guilt of disunity. But, brethren, we
must acknowledge our own guilt as well and this we have
been somewhat less than willing to do. If Rome attempts
to renew herself in full view of the whole world, nothing
less is required of us. . . . And we must admit our share
in initiating and perpetuating the schism of the 16th century. . . . If the Pope will undertake Christian amplifica-
tion of his own real image, we Anglicans and Protestants
should consider most prayerfully our relationship to him.
We should, I for one believe, acknowledge him as the
Chief Pastor of the Christian Family and we should joy-
fully acclaim him as the Holy Father in God of the Universal Church. Such a move on our part, taken now, is far
more important than our current consultation on the reunion of several American denominations. The truth is, we
need the Pope because in this perilous age we need some
one symbolically potent bishop to give expression to the
Word of the Lord for our day. We need someone to say,
as chief pastor in Christ, that the worldwide community of
Christians must exert its massive power to halt war and
conflict in the world. We need a chief pastor who will lead
us in the fight against poverty and the powerlessness of
peoples in the earth. *We need a Holy Father.* We need a
Father who can speak and witness to the whole human
race in such words as those contained in John's *Pacem in
terris* or Paul's *The Progress of Peoples* and, quite simply,
as the presence among us of the Fisherman. . . . We

today may no longer even think of the reunion of Christendom without the Papacy. For a long time we have harbored the illusion that reunion would come by first uniting Anglicans, Protestants, and the Orthodox. Pope John has changed all of this . . . changed it all, I believe, by his faithful listening to the winds of the Holy Spirit. Our response to his response should be to seek ways by which spiritually (if not organically) we may return to a Papacy renewed and reformed. This, in my judgment, would in no way constitute a denial of our Reformation loyalties, for Rome herself (including the Papacy) has accepted the principle of continued reformation in the Church.

If the remarks of Bishops Moorman and Myers may be seen as illustrative of the observations that some members of the Anglican episcopate have been willing to offer in the wake of the Second Vatican Council, it is no less true that the modern ecumenical climate has witnessed a more favorable view of the papacy among some leading Anglican theologians. The ground for it was laid as early as 1958 by Professor Eric Mascall in his book *The Recovery of Unity*, probably the most classical modern Anglican appreciation of the papal office. Mascall pointed out that acceptance of the papal claims would involve the acceptance of four propositions forming a logical sequence, all of which seemed plausible to him except the last:

1. That Christ conferred on St. Peter a primacy over the Church and the other apostles.
2. That this primacy was transmissible to Peter's successors.
3. That Peter's successors are the bishops of Rome.
4. That this primacy involves the absolute supremacy in government and teaching which is commonly claimed by the popes and commonly (as of 1958!)[30] expounded by Roman Catholic theologians.[31]

Several other leading contemporary Anglican theologians have echoed these views, although they have been less ready than Mascall apparently was to accord a primacy to the successors of Peter on strictly biblical or historical grounds alone. In 1965 the distinguished biblical scholar and Anglican observer at Vatican II, Professor Frederick C. Grant, wrote: "The main obstacle to Christian reunion is not papal infallibility or even the papal primacy, which could be adequately defended on historical or pragmatic grounds on the basis of practical needs for centralized government and administration of the Christian church. *The real obstacle is the violence done to the New Testament in every attempt to defend the primacy as an institution dating from the first century and founded by Christ himself.*"[32] It was this, rather than a papal primacy as such, to which Grant objected. "Far from discarding it, or disregarding it, and in spite of the false claims often made for it and the flimsy exegesis its apologists have too often employed, the papacy is one of the most priceless elements in the Christian heritage. Reformed and restored to a pristine state in which, among the church's leaders, it should be once more first among equals (*primus inter pares*), rather than a monarchical sovereignty, the papacy might very well become the acknowledged leader, guide, and chief of the whole Christian church, and the greatest influence for good in all the world."[33]

John MacQuarrie, now Lady Margaret Professor of Divinity at Oxford, picked up themes that represent a blending of the positions of Mascall and Grant in his *Principles of Christian Theology* (1966). St. Peter, he affirms, did have a "certain primacy" among the apostles. Whether or not this primacy, and any special attendant prerogatives, passed over to his successors in the see of Rome is not easy for MacQuarrie to answer, but is in his opinion no more obscure a question than the rise of the New Testament canon, the development of the sacraments, or the emergence of a definitely structured ministry. "If we are prepared to call the latter three 'apostolic,' should we deny the title to the papacy?"[34] The papacy was, moreover, in MacQuarrie's view just as invaluable as the other three in nurturing the Church and in preserving its unity and integrity through the early centuries. MacQuarrie flatly rejects any notion of "infallibility" in the Church or papacy, but he does write approvingly of the notion of a papal primacy within—not additional to, or outside of, or above—the episcopate, as something which "belongs to the fullness of the Church."[35]

Eric Kemp, the historian of medieval English canon law and now bishop of Chichester, in a paper prepared in 1967 for the Anglican/Roman Catholic Joint Preparatory Commission, gave the opinion that "most Anglicans would have no difficulty in giving to the Papacy the kind of appellate jurisdiction assigned to it by the Council of Sardica. Where they would find difficulty is in being asked to acknowledge that the Pope has by divine commission the right to intervene with ordinary authority in the affairs of local churches, to restrict their bishops in their pastoral office, or to suppress local hierarchies."[36] And the liturgiologist Massey Shepherd has taken a similar stand (1972) in observing that, even given the possible resolution of doctrinal differences such as infallibility and the Mariological definitions, it is most unlikely that the Anglican churches would abandon the participation of their laity in all levels of decision-making and the non-veto of a primate over collegial decisions of the episcopate. "Anglicans," says Shepherd, "could accept the Pope as servant of the unity of the Church and its universal primate, but not the statement of *Lumen gentium* (ch. III, sec. 22) that 'the Roman Pontiff has full, supreme, and universal power over the Church.' "[37]

And again in 1972, Archbishop Ramsey at Graymoor, New York, reiterated with new urgency the view that seems to have been his consistent stand ever since 1936:

> It seems to me entirely acceptable that the spirit of truth reigns in the Church, and that when the Church collectively is guided into a common mind, it is for the Pope, as the presiding genius, to declare what that mind is.[38]

At the most official level is the periodical worldwide meeting of Anglican bishops known as the Lambeth Conference, whose decisions, although not binding, do carry great weight and persuasive force for Anglicans. The (latest) 1968 Conference moved slightly beyond previous ones in making these very balanced but friendly remarks in its final statement on the papacy.[39]

As a result of the emphasis placed on collegiality at the Second Vatican Council, the status of bishops in the Roman Catholic Church was in great measure enhanced though the teaching of the First Vatican Council on the infallibility and immediate and universal jurisdiction of the Pope was unaffected. We are unable to accept this teaching as it is commonly understood today. The relationships between the Pope and the episcopal college, of which he is a member, are, however, still being clarified, and are subject to development. We recall the statement made in the Lambeth Conference of 1908, and repeated in 1920 and 1930, "that there can be no fulfillment of the Divine purpose in any scheme of reunion which does not ultimately include the great Latin Church of the West, with which our history has been so closely associated in the past, and to which we are still bound by many ties of common faith and tradition." We recognize the Papacy as an historic reality whose developing role requires deep reflection and joint study by all concerned for the unity of the whole Body of Christ.

It has been suggested that this statement might have been even stronger had not the papal encyclical *Humanae Vitae* appeared on July 29, 1968 at the time of the debate.[40] Whether or not this is so, it is certainly true that the first draft of the Lambeth statement was even more positive in its gestures toward the papal see:

The papacy is an historic reality whose claims must be

carefully weighed in any scheme for the reunion of Christendom. Within the whole college of bishops and in ecumenical councils it is evident that there must be a president whose office involves a personal concern for the
affairs of the whole Church. This president might most fit-
tingly be the occupant of the historic see of Rome. Although as we understand them at present we are unable to
accept the claims of the papacy to infallibility and immediate and universal jurisdiction, we believe that a considerable majority of Anglicans would be prepared to accept
the Pope as having a primacy of love, implying both honour and service, in a renewed and reunited Church as
would seem right on both historical and pragmatic
grounds.

Even with the statement that Lambeth 1968 did finally adopt,
however, there was no way that this Conference could have
ended with the regrets about Rome that had been expressed at
the Conference of 1908: "Under present circumstances it is
useless to consider the question of possible intercommunion
with our brethren of that Communion in view of the fact that
no such proposal would be entertained but on conditions which
it would be impossible for us to accept."[41] The years since 1908
had seen too many changes in just this direction for such a
statement to be possible again in 1968 or the foreseeable future.

No historical survey would be complete, finally, without
some note of what Anglicans have been willing to say in recent
ecumenical conversations on the subject. It is generally known
that the papacy, under the broader question of authority in the
Church, is now the topic of formal discussions at the highest
official level between Anglicans and Roman Catholics. As of
the present writing there is yet no final agreed statement on
this question from the Anglican/Roman Catholic International
Commission, but some indication of the direction in which the
Anglican members of that Commission have been willing to go

may be gleaned from the preliminary working reports of that Commission, known as the Venice Papers, published in 1971:

> Any view of the papal authority likely to commend itself to Anglicans would have to make clear that a notion of "primacy of service" was central. Precise theological definition might well for many be less fundamental. It is unlikely that many Anglicans would be content with the 1870 definition as it has been expounded up to the present time in the Roman Catholic Church.

> Anglicans believe that the commandment given to Peter is inherited in a general sense by the whole Church (to which the power to bind and loose is entrusted by the Lord in Mt. 18) and in a particular sense by every bishop of the *ecclesia catholica*. The Petrine duty of shepherding the flock is fulfilled by every act of the teaching ministry of the Church, whether exercised by individual bishops in their own dioceses, or by bishops in council. As a bishop of the universal Church, the bishop of Rome certainly inherits this task, though not in such an exclusive sense that he possesses it as no other bishop or council of bishops can. When he is seen to speak with the voice of the universal Church, he speaks a truly Petrine utterance. But this function does not exclusively inhere in the office of bishop of Rome as such. Anglicans attach great importance to the Lord's commission (or commissions) to St. Peter; but they cannot accept either explicit or implicit assumptions that the Petrine text of Mt. 16 can be transferred to the bishops of Rome, or that "the Petrine office" and "the Papacy" are virtually synonymous and interchangeable terms.

> In preference to infallibility, Anglicans have preferred to speak of the Church's indefectibility. The Lord has promised to be with his people to the end of the world. The

Spirit is given to guide the Church into all truth. Yet the empirical Church remains a community of men who are subject to blindness and sinfulness. Therefore any given definition of authority is open to the possibility of error, so that even general councils (which, for Anglicans, remain the highest authority under the word of God) are capable of onesidedness, inadequacy or other error (as, for example, Ariminum 359 and Ephesus 449). Yet the Church is indwelt by the Spirit and is not only safeguarded from a total and final departure from the truth but also granted continual correction. . . .

If there are substantial Anglican hesitations about the papacy as such, it would not be unreasonable to say that these generally have far more to do with the actual exercise of papal authority (at various periods in history) than with the papacy itself or the subtleties of definition. . . .

It may indeed be possible to envisage a papal primacy of honor and service, but such a primacy can ultimately be justified only as a useful historical development within the life of the Church.[42]

From all of the above evidence, therefore, I want to suggest that the Anglican stance toward the papacy since the sixteenth century has evolved from that of "anti-papal" to one which today may at least be called "non-papal." No exhaustive historical study of this evolution exists. Undoubtedly there are some Anglican writers even today who take a more negative attitude, and of course there is no statistical or numerical tabulation of viewpoints. But I do think the above survey indicates not only a shift from the sixteenth century but also a contemporary Anglican attitude of openness, of genuine interest, and at times of even more than mere neutrality. There exists, in classical Anglican apologetic and in contemporary Anglican theology, a considerable body of positive opinion favorable to some sort of papal primacy.

What Sort of Papacy
Would Not Be Acceptable to Anglicans?

Moving from the historical survey to a contemporary estimate, I next want to sketch out what sort of papacy might,
and what sort might not, be acceptable to Anglicans today.
Lest my foregoing historical survey seem to suggest that all
Anglicanism is rapidly moving in an entirely pro-papal direction, I now want to indicate the sort of papacy that I think
would *not* be acceptable to most Anglicans today. Needless to
say, I can only speak with finality for myself, but I do think
certain final limits, or *termini ad quem*, for the majority of
Anglicans emerge from the foregoing survey. I intend to be
straightforward and at times even blunt in listing these, because
I believe no service is done for the ecumenical cause by gloss-
ing them over.

1. A concept of papal infallibility, at least as it has been
defined by Vatican I (1870), Vatican II (1964), and the declaration *Mysterium Ecclesiae*, ratified by Pope Paul VI in 1973,
must be ruled out. Its meaning within the Roman Catholic understanding of Christianity has undoubtedly been a positive one
in the lives and faith of many adherents, but it remains *the* doctrine most peculiarly odd about the Roman Church when
viewed from the outside. A good survey of the logical, theological, and philosophical objections to this concept by Professor
Carolyn Craft appeared in a recent issue of the *Anglican Theological Review*.[43] Further doubts about it have certainly been
raised by recent research into its historical origins, and Roman
Catholic scholars vary widely in their interpretation of it.[44]
Whatever meaning it may have for them is best left for them to
debate, but it must be understood in ecumenical dialogue that
Anglicans generally cannot accept the infallibility definitions of
1870, 1964, and 1973, no matter how much respect we may
have for the papal *primacy*.

2. Universal ordinary jurisdiction, whereby the bishop of
Rome may intervene directly in the affairs of any diocese or

regional body of bishops with full and supreme power above the authority of the local bishop or regional episcopal college, is also a prerogative of the present papacy that is unacceptable to most Anglicans. We could never, for example, accord him the power to appoint our bishops, nor reserve to him the right to sanction or withhold their consecrations. The strictures of Professor MacQuarrie, Bishop Kemp, and Professor Shepherd, as well as the Venice Papers, all of which I have cited above, make this clear. The problem is that whereas Anglicans tend to regard episcopal consecration as primarily constituting the head of a local church, Roman Catholics tend to think of the new bishop as first of all "a member of the episcopal college succeeding the apostolic college in the ministry of teaching, jurisdiction, and order."[45] The implications of this problem are indicated by the fact that when Pope Paul VI concluded the October 1974 Synod of Bishops by rejecting much of its work, he even took pains to emphasize that papal "intervention" within the college of bishops "cannot be reduced only to extraordinary circumstances. No: we say with trepidation, by reason of the responsibility that falls upon us, that the Successor of Peter is and remains the ordinary Pastor of the Church in her unity and entirety."[46]

3. The claim that even the papal *primacy* is an institution dating from the first century and founded by Christ himself would also be widely rejected on grounds of biblical and historical scholarship, as the quoted remarks of the late Professor Grant and the Venice Papers indicate. There are, however, at least some signs, in the Venice Papers and in the recently published volume on papal primacy from the American Lutheran/Catholic dialogue, that some Anglican scholars may be able to see in the New Testament texts a *Petrine* primacy, and in the early fathers a *Roman* primacy, of responsibility and service, of which the single most notable representative has been the Roman bishop.[47]

4. The absolute supremacy of the Roman pontiff over an ecumenical council, as defined, for example, by Canons 222,

227, and 228 of the current Code of Canon Law in the Roman Catholic Church—that the pope alone may convoke an ecumenical council, decide its business, suspend or dissolve it, promulgate its decrees, and that appeal may not be made from him to it—is a far greater power than the sort of presidency within an ecumenical council that most Anglicans *might* be willing to accord the Roman bishop.[48]

5. The constant agreement and defense, not just of the pope as leader and elder brother in Christ, but even of the pope's opinions and teachings on virtually every question of doctrine, is a demand placed upon every bishop of the Roman Catholic obedience that almost no Anglican bishop would accept. In particular, the two following stipulations issued as recently as 1973 in the Vatican's *Directory on the Pastoral Ministry of Bishops*[49] may be cited:

—In matters of faith and morals, the bishop considers it his duty to think with the Church and to agree with the Roman pontiff.

—A bishop also adheres in devoted and religious allegiance to the pope's ordinary magisterium, and by written and spoken word and other means of communication spreads, supports, and, if the need arises, defends it in his diocese.

Some, perhaps many, Roman Catholic bishops may have rather minimizing ways of interpreting these passages, but they are simply not the sort of rules that a typical Anglican bishop would readily enter upon, even for the sake of unity.

6. The apparent requirement, reaffirmed both in Vatican II and in *Mysterium Ecclesiae*, that even the laity are expected to assent and submit, both in will and in mind, to the teachings of the Roman pontiff even when he is not speaking *ex cathedra*, is a demand to which most Anglican laypersons would not give their assent. Some, perhaps many, of the Roman Catholic faithful may have rather minimizing ways of interpreting this

requirement also, but there is no way that the great majority of Anglican laity, even for the sake of unity, would agree to bind themselves under such a stipulation as the following text from Vatican II: "In matters of faith and morals, the bishops speak in the name of Christ, and the faithful (*fideles*) are to accept (*concurrere*) their teaching and adhere (*adhaerere debent*) to it with a religious assent (*obsequio*) of soul. This religious submission (*obsequium*) of will and of mind (*voluntatis et intellectus*) must be shown in a special way to the authentic teaching authority of the Roman pontiff, even when he is not speaking *ex cathedra*."[50]

7. The so-called "Uniate" solution for reunion with the papal see, whereby on analogy with certain Eastern churches there would become an international "Anglican Rite" under ultimate Roman obedience but with its own canon law, particular form of worship, and English language and tradition, with the archbishop of Canterbury as patriarch or possibly a member of the College of Cardinals, is a model that has appealed to some Anglicans at first thought but is generally rejected by most after more careful consideration.[51] The problems of infallibility and universal ordinary jurisdiction remain, the question of how bishops would be chosen is raised, the phenomenon of already very similar contemporary Anglican and Roman liturgical rites—at least in America—is overlooked, and the confusion of parallel episcopal hierarchies is not solved. A solution more congenial to Anglicans might be a relationship to the Roman Catholic Church similar to that which the Anglican Communion has held with the Old Catholics and the so-called "Wider Episcopal Fellowship," but that relationship makes no provision for the papal primacy with which we are now concerned.

What Sort of Papacy Might Anglicans Be Prepared To Accept?

If the above, then, are the contours of the sort of papacy that Anglicans today would probably *not* accept, we may next move to consider what sort they *might* accept. First, I think we have to ask some questions of each side which, if answered positively, will provide the clarifications necessary for a basic agreement on the papal primacy. As Fr. Herbert Ryan has suggested for Roman Catholics, their first question is whether or not it is possible to have a plurality of colleges of bishops within the one *communio* or *koinonia* of the Church.[52] Can Roman Catholics see themselves recognizing the autonomous churches of the Anglican Communion as sister churches within the one fellowship of Christ's body, and even concelebrating and receiving the sacrament of Holy Communion with Anglicans, if Anglicans still have an independent doctrinal existence of their own, not absorbed under the Roman obedience, and remain unable to accept the sort of papal doctrine and jurisdiction—still apparently so fundamental to Roman Catholic belief —that I have sketched above in my seven points of objection? Is it possible that, just as the centuries since the Reformation have seen the development of a rather centralized and authoritarian sort of papal power within the Roman Communion as it has grown on its own, so the time now since Vatican II may begin to see the concept of papal primacy expand to include some sort of benevolent service, of pastoral responsibility, extended to groups of Christians not within the innermost circle of Roman Catholic dogma and obedience? Might the particular Roman dogmas proclaimed during this period of mutual separation—the immaculate conception, assumption, and infallibility—be *not* expected as an absolute requirement for unity with the churches that have grown up outside this development?[53] If Roman Catholics are to take seriously the possibilities for corporate reunion (and not just individual conversion), envisaged by Vatican II's *Decree on Ecumenism*, then within which of the Christian Churches that embody some "protestant" elements are they likely to find a *more* positive attitude toward the papacy than among Anglicans?[54]

For the Anglican side, the question is whether *any* sort of papal primacy, the concept of a single personal focus of unity and authority, however defined, within the Church can now be seen and officially acknowledged as necessary or at least desirable? The great American Anglican scholastic theologian F. J. Hall wrote in 1908: "The papal see must adjust its positions and methods, so far as they are of human growth, to the changing conditions, the advancing civilization, and the increasing spiritual intelligence of the people on whose allegiance its continuance absolutely depends. It must do this or die. . . . We believe that it . . . has a future, by reason of such readjustment of attitude, with which we must someday reckon."[55] At the 1930 Lambeth Conference, in response to a question from the Orthodox as to where the highest authority of the Church lay, still the Anglicans felt moved to deny "any idea of a central authority, other than councils of bishops."[56] But Anglican attitudes to the papacy, and the Roman Catholic conception of it, have changed considerably since then, as my historical survey indicates, and the question of a papal primacy *within* an ecumenical council, *within* the college of bishops, and hence *within* the Church, is now an open one for us. The day of reckoning predicted by Professor Hall has now begun. Given the historical development of a more neutral, and even positive, attitude on the part of many Anglicans toward some sort of papal primacy, we are now being asked to spell out what it might mean. We, as Anglicans, are now beginning to sense within ourselves, as do the Lutherans, "a growing awareness of the necessity of a specific ministry to serve the Church's unity and universal mission."[57]

If the answers to the questions I have posed above are generally in the affirmative, then the following is a sketch of the sort of papacy that I think would be generally acceptable to Anglicans. We would be willing, on the basis of historical contingencies but not by divine right, to recognize the see of Rome as the first (prime) see of Christendom, and to accord its occupants a primacy of leadership and honor, but not of doctrine or power. We would be willing to accord this not because of any scholarly conviction that a primacy or infallibility was conferred by Christ upon Peter and his successors as the bishops of Rome, but rather because of the pre-eminent place that the

Roman see and its occupants came to hold in the worldwide
Church, much in the same way as Canterbury and its occupants have come to be accorded the traditional place of
honor within the Anglican Communion. I think we could agree
with the joint statement of the American Lutheran/Catholic
dialogue that a "Petrine function" in the New Testament is
discernible, which serves to promote unity, communication, assistance, and collaboration within the Church, and that the single most notable representative of this ministry has been (we
would add "and should be again, within fixed limits") the bishop of Rome.[58] We would thus be willing to speak of Rome,
with the words that St. Ignatius of Antioch uses of that see and
no other, as "the church which presides in love."[59] And we
would, for this reason, be willing to look upon the Roman bishop as the "first among equals" (*primus inter pares*) in the
worldwide episcopal council, to declare its results as the mind
of the Church, and together with his staff at Rome to lead the
worldwide Church on a regular basis much as the Presiding
Bishop does on a regular basis for the Episcopal Church in the
U.S.A. The pope would thus, in a way that is both pragmatic
and sacramental, serve as the single personal focus for the
worldwide unity and mission of the Church of God. He would,
by virtue of his very responsibilities as moderator, coordinator,
and facilitator of unity between churches in communion with
each other, have a certain defined functional and pastoral authority, more than that of a chairman but less than the "supreme" power" of a *pontifex maximus*. This authority, as any
bishop or other person responsible for leadership, prophecy,
and teaching in the Church well knows, would always be subject to the temptations and charges of domination and misuse,
but this authority would be limited, subject to review by the
whole Church in some sort of due process, and would not extend to initiative in doctrine.

This much, then, I believe most Anglicans—at least in the
Episcopal Church of the U.S.A.—would be willing to accord a
pope, and I think they would be willing to live in communion
with this understanding of him alongside of their brothers and

sisters in the Roman Communion who have many more extensive beliefs about his doctrinal and jurisidictional authority. He
would not have the rights over our bishops or laypersons that I
have objected to in points five and six earlier, but, on the other
hand, I do think most Anglicans would be quite prepared to accord his opinions generally the sort of reception urged by Cardinal Dearden of Detroit and the National Conference of
Catholic Bishops at the time of the *Humanae Vitae* crisis: "To
receive with sincerity what he has taught, to study it carefully,
and to form their consciences in its light."[60] The limits to this
sort of papal primacy, of course, would have to be set down on
paper, and it would be desirable to adopt one or more titles—
slogans, really—to summarize what we have come to believe
about him. I myself would be inclined to favor the three
phrases employed by Professor Massey Shepherd ("Servant of
the unity of the Church and its universal primate"), by Bishop
Kilmer Myers ("Chief Pastor of the Christian Family"), and
by the first draft of Lambeth 1968 ("Primacy of love, implying
both honour and service"). To take this much of a step, then, I
think would be consistent with the historical evolution I have
already outlined, and I think both our Communions would be
the richer for it.

Next Steps

If Anglicans come to see the above sort of limited papal
primacy as being desirable for them, then what might be the
next steps that lie ahead? I see two sorts:

A. *Official Agreements*

1. First, there would have to be "an official and explicit
affirmation of mutual recognition from the highest authorities
of each Communion" as has already been proposed in the

Malta Report (1968) of the Anglican/Roman Catholic Joint
Preparatory Commission:

> It would acknowledge that both Communions are at one
> in the faith that the Church is founded upon the revelation
> of God the Father, made known to us in the Person and
> work of Jesus Christ, who is present through the Holy
> Spirit in the Scriptures and his Church, and is the only
> Mediator between God and man, the ultimate Authority
> for all our doctrine. Each accepts the basic truths set forth
> in the ecumenical Creeds and the common tradition of the
> ancient Church, although neither Communion is tied to a
> positive acceptance of all the beliefs and devotional prac-
> tices of the other.[61]

2. Paul VI has admitted that the pope himself is "unquestionably the most serious obstacle on the path of ecumenism,"[62] and I think the other outstanding doctrinal differences,
apart from the pope, should be solved in a mutually acceptable
way first. The Windsor (1971) and Canterbury (1973) Statements (possibly revised) on the Eucharist and on Ordination,
topics that have divided us in the past, would have to move
from being simply agreed reports *to* our churches from the
Anglican/Roman Catholic International Commission to a
status of becoming doctrinal agreements *between* our churches.
The Roman Catholics would have to be satisfied with traditional Anglican understandings of the immaculate conception,
assumption, and infallibility, and Anglicans would have to
come to some sort of terms with the 1896 Bull on the invalidity
of Anglican orders.[63] Both sides, moreover, would probably
want to insure some sort of protection from possible future
decisions of the one side unlikely to win immediate acceptance
among the faithful of the other church, such as the co-redemp-
tion of Mary or the ordination of women.
3. Then a basic agreed statement about the papal primacy, perhaps of the sort that I have proposed above, should

be prepared by a joint international commission, and it should set forth clearly the kind of authority and responsibility, as well as the jurisdictional and doctrinal limits, that Anglicans are prepared to accord the pope, together with the degree of sacramental sharing and *koinonia* that Roman Catholics would be prepared to accord their Anglican brothers and sisters in such an arrangement. Perhaps some sort of church union in concentric circles might be envisaged, with the pope in the center, the Roman Catholic Church according him supreme power of doctrine and jurisdiction in the first or inner circle, and in a second or outer circle the Anglican Communion accepting him with the limits I have suggested above and calling him by the titles that Professor Shepherd, Bishop Myers, and the first draft of Lambeth 1968 have employed. The question of Anglican participation in a future ecumenical council, and of whether Anglican bishops would participate in future papal elections, would also have to be determined. Any such agreement, for Anglicans, would have to take into account the principle of Anglican regional autonomy: it would have to be discussed at a Lambeth Conference, and the question would have to be decided whether all, or only some, of the independent churches of the Anglican Communion were going to enter upon this arrangement. The probability that the eventual visible reunion of all of the separated churches can only take place gradually and in a somewhat random way in various regions of the world, "at different paces in different places," would have to be faced directly by both sides and might indicate a reunion process with different timetables for different national areas.

B. *Practical Matters*

Several practical steps could also be taken, many from the Anglican side, and most of them even prior to the official agreements I have suggested above.

1. Anglicans could begin praying for the pope in their li-

turgies, inserting his name, and perhaps one of the titles suggested, in the eucharistic prayer of intercession—e.g., "for Paul
VI, Chief Pastor of the Christian Family, for John our Presiding Bishop . . . we pray to you, O Lord." It is possible that the
Episcopal Church's General Convention or Liturgical Commission might make such a proposal, although there is certainly
nothing to stop individual parishes right now from beginning to
pray for the pope in this way—and some already do so.

2. Anglican bishops might ask to be put on the same mailing list as Roman Catholic bishops, to receive all routine non-
confidential mailings sent from the Holy Father and his Curia
to all bishops throughout the world under his obedience. Individual bishops could certainly ask for this on their own, but either the Lambeth Conference of Anglican bishops or the
American House of Bishops of the Episcopal Church might
make such a request officially and corporately (and offer to
pay the costs of additional printing and mailing). Such an exchange of information would be *one* tangible way in which
Anglican bishops could test the value of a papal primacy and
form their own estimate of the desirability of having a single
personal focus of leadership for the Church's unity and mission. The new 116-page *Directory on the Pastoral Ministry of
Bishops*, for example, which I have already mentioned above,
contains very much that would be of considerable interest,
value, and use to our own bishops. Similar exchanges of mailing, likewise, could be arranged for diocesan ecumenical com-
mittees, liturgical chairmen, etc.

3. Another practical step would be for the national Ecumenical Offices of the Episcopal and Roman Catholic
Churches, respectively, in New York and Washington, to pre-
pare a list of "paired bishops," whereby each Anglican bishop
would be paired with a Roman bishop within a contiguous ter-
ritory and the two would be encouraged to meet with each
other regularly, not only to share their experiences of *episcope*,
but in particular for the Roman bishop to explain to his Anglican counterpart what value *he* finds in the mailings and other

services performed as the Petrine ministry of the pope at Rome.

4. The official Lutheran/Catholic Dialogue in the U.S.A. has already produced a splendid 255-page paperback, *Papal Primacy and the Universal Church*,[64] containing their common agreed statement about the papal primacy (not infallibility) together with the scholarly papers that helped them reach these conclusions. This could be taken as the basic text for joint lay and clergy study groups throughout the Anglican and Roman Catholic Churches, and reports could be prepared on the extent of endorsement it receives among us. In this way Anglicans might join their brothers and sisters of the Roman Communion in reformulating a concept of papal primacy for our time that is more biblical, more pastoral, and less legalistic. Fr. Avery Dulles points out that such a reformulation of Vatican I on the papal primacy, "to correspond better to the concerns, the linguistic usage, and the general outlook of our own day," is in fact already being called for by several Roman Catholic authorities,[65] and there is every reason why this should be done from an ecumenical perspective.

In all of these ways, then, Anglicans and Roman Catholics might jointly arrive at a convergence of belief on the question of a papal primacy of the sort that seems appropriate for our time, given the diversity of viewpoints that are inevitable in our pluralistic churches of the present and future. Not all Anglicans are yet convinced that the Church *needs* any sort of pope or that the Gospel even allows for one. Can we see, asks Archbishop Ramsey, a papal primacy that depends upon and expresses the general mind of all the bishops and the organic authority of the whole body, as being a legitimate development of the Gospel? I suggest that our answer can only come from cautious investigation of the sort that I have proposed above: let us begin with the practical matters and at the same time continue a dialogue about what the official agreement might look like. "The tests of a true development," wrote Ramsey, "are whether it bears witness to the Gospel, whether it expresses the general consciousness of the Christians, and whether it serves the organic unity of the body in all its parts."[66] Is it possible for us as Anglicans to reach an organic relationship in communion with the pope of Rome that meets these tests? I think so.

NOTES

1. A. G. Dickens and Dorothy Carr, *The Reformation in England to the Accession of Elizabeth I* (London 1967), 46-89; A. G. Dickens, *The English Reformation* (London 1964), 113-122.

2. See, for example, J. J. Scarisbrick, "Clerical Taxation in England 1485-1547," *Journal of Ecclesiastical History* XI (1960), 41-54; W. E. Lunt, *Financial Relations of the Papacy with England 1327-1534* (Cambridge, Mass., 1962), ch. VIII; E. J. Bicknell, *A Theological Introduction to the Thirty-Nine Articles of the Church of England*, rev. H. J. Carpenter (London 1955), 426-29.

3. See, e.g., J. W. Gray, "Canon Law in England—Some Reflections on the Stubbs-Maitland Controversy," *Studies in Church History* III, ed. G. J. Cuming (London 1966), 48-68; D. Hay, "The Church of England in the Later Middle Ages," *History* LIII:177 (February 1968) 35-50; and *The English Church and The Papacy in the Middle Ages*, ed. C. H. Lawrence (London 1965).

4. T. M. Powicke, *The Reformation in England* (London 1941), ch. 1; Dickens, *op. cit.*, p. 107 and n. 22; P. M. Dawley, *John Whitgift and the English Reformation* (N.Y. 1954), 1-24.

5. Glanmor Williams, *Reformation Views of Church History* (London 1970), esp. p. 27.

6. See, for example, the assertions in the Bishops' Book of 1537; P. Hughes, *The Reformation in England* (London 1963), II, 30-35.

7. Cf. G. J. Cuming, *A History of Anglican Liturgy* (London 1969), 54.

8. *The First and Second Prayer Books of Edward VI*, introd. by E.C.S. Gibson (Everyman's Library, London 1910), 232, 362. This clause was, however, omitted from the Litany during the reign of Mary Tudor. W. P. Haugaard, "The English Litany from Henry to Elizabeth," *Anglican Theological Review* LI:3 (July 1969), 179, 188-9.

9. Bicknell, *op. cit.*, 11, 14, 420ff; M. H. Shepherd, Jr., *The Oxford American Prayer Book Commentary* (New York 1950), 601, 610.

10. Ed. J. E. Booty (Ithaca 1963), 91-93, cf. 25-26. See also H. R. McAdoo, *The Spirit of Anglicanism: A Survey of Anglican Theological Method in the Seventeenth Century* (N.Y. 1965), chs. IX and X, for discussion of this approach.

11. W. M. Southgate, *John Jewel and the Problem of Doctrinal Authority* (Cambridge, Mass., 1962), 125-127.

12. Hughes, *op. cit.*, III, 166-67, and cf. p. 77.

13. R. A. Crofts, "The Defense of the Elizabethan Church: Jewel, Hooker, and James I," *Anglican Theological Review* LIV:1 (January 1972), 24. P. E. More and F. L. Cross, eds., *Anglicanism* (London 1935), 69-71.

14. For a start see G. H. Tavard, *The Quest for Catholicity* (N.Y. 1964).

15. More and Cross, *op. cit.*, 6-7.

16. The learned Hooker is, by contrast with Jewel on this point, considerably more judicious; *Ecclesiastical Polity* (1594), bk. IV. Richard Field, *Of the Church* (1606-10), and Richard Crakenthorpe, *Defensio Ecclesiae Anglicanae* (1625), are also noteworthy examples of the emerging Anglican position.

17. A. M. Allchin, "The Place of Anglicanism," in *Oecumenica: An Annual Symposium of Ecumenical Research*, ed. F. W. Kantzenbach and V. Vajta (Minneapolis 1966), 86.

18. More and Cross, *op. cit.*, 7, 55.

19. *Ibid.*, 57, 65-66.

20. *Ibid.*, 63, 66.

21. *A Discourse Against the Infallibility of the Roman Church* (1634?). *The Works of W. Chillingworth, M.A.* . . . twelfth ed., London 1836, 683ff.

22. *A Dissuasive from Popery* (1664). *The Whole Works of the Right Rev. Jeremy Taylor* . . ., (ed.) Reginald Heber. Third ed. of the collected works, London, 1839; e.g., vol. X, 177ff., 297, 331ff., vol. XI, 665-67.

23. (1676). More and Cross, *op. cit.*, 72.

24. (1680). *Ibid.*, 68.

25. These and the following three views are quoted from J. C. Dickinson, "Papal Authority—The Background," in *Infallibility in the Church*, ed. M. D. Goulder (London 1968), 50-51.

26. London 1936, 227-28.

27. London 1957, 125-26.

28. *Church Times* (London), 8 July 1966 and 10 February 1967. Two quotations have been conflated and the italicized words in parentheses supplied.

29. *Holy Cross Magazine*, (West Park, N.Y.), July 1967, 2-5; cf. *American Church News* (Pelham Manor, N.Y.), September 27, 1967, and *The Little Chronicle* (Mt. Sinai, L.I., N.Y.), LII:2, November 1970.

30. For some developments since 1958 in the diverse ways in which papal primacy is expounded by Roman Catholic theologians, see pp. 151-159 of my essay "Papacy in the Church of the Future—An Anglican Perspective," in *Episcopalians and Roman Catholics: Can They Ever Get Together?*, ed. H. J. Ryan and J. R. Wright (Graymoor, N.Y., 1972).

31. E. L. Mascall, *The Recovery of Unity* (London, 1958), 197, 201. Mascall reaffirmed these four points, as well as his demurrer from the last of them, in *The Tablet* (London), 31 July 1971, 739.

32. F. C. Grant, *Rome and Reunion* (N.Y. 1965), 7. Italics added.

33 *Ibid.*, 144.

34. A similar question is asked by Professor Reginald Fuller at the end of his essay "The Ministry in the New Testament" in Ryan and Wright, *op. cit.*, 103: "We can only justify our institutions in terms of legitimate development. This applies to priesthood, episcopacy, and succession. Could it also, for Anglicans, legitimate the development of the primacy of the Bishop of Rome?"

35. J. MacQuarrie, *Principles of Christian Theology* (N.Y. 1966), 369-71; cf. *Concilium*, vol. 54, *Post-Ecumenical Christianity*, ed. H. Küng (N.Y. 1970), 49.

36. Quoted from *Anglican/Roman Catholic Dialogue: The Work of the Preparatory Commission*, ed. A.C. Clark and C. Davey (London 1974), 18.

37. *Concilium*, vol. 74, *The Plurality of Ministries*, ed. H. Küng and W. Kasper (N.Y. 1971), 95-96.

38. *Pilgrim from Canterbury Visits Friars at Graymoor* (Garrison, N.Y., 1972), 19. For similar statements cf. the *Church Times* (London), 29 November 1967: "I don't think that Christendom as a whole would accept the Pope as infallible in defining faith and morals. But I do think Christendom as a whole might accept the Pope as presiding bishop among the bishops of the world"; also in J. B. Simpson, *The Hundredth Archbishop of Canterbury* (N.Y. 1962), 162: "I would be willing to accept the Pope as a presiding bishop, but not as infallible. I would be willing to call him *primus inter pares*, first among equals."

39. *The Lambeth Conference 1968: Resolutions and Reports* (London 1968), 137-8.

40. *Herder Correspondence* VI:1 (January 1969), 27; *Concilium*, vol. 54, *Post-Ecumenical Christianity*, ed. H. Küng (N.Y. 1970), 47-48; J. B. Simpson and E. M. Story, *The Long Shadows of Lambeth X* (N.Y. 1969), 229-233. The 1968 Conference met from July 25 to August 25. It is interesting to compare the effect of the 1870 infallibility decree upon the statement of the second Lambeth Conference of 1878: "The fact that a solemn protest is raised in so many Churches and Christian communities throughout the world against the usurpations of the See of Rome, and against the novel doctrines promulgated by its authority, is a subject for thankfulness to Almighty God. All sympathy is due from the Anglican Church to the Churches and individuals protesting against these errors, and labouring, it may be, under special difficulties from the assaults of unbelief as well as from the pretensions of Rome. . . . It is therefore our duty to warn the faithful that the act done by the Bishop of Rome, in the Vatican Council, in the year 1870—whereby he asserted a supremacy over all men in matters both of faith and morals, on the ground of an assumed infallibility—was an invasion of the attributes of the Lord Jesus Christ." Quoted from W. H. Van de Pol, *Anglicanism in Ecumenical Perspective* (Pittsburgh 1965), 42.

41. *Conference of Bishops of the Anglican Communion Holden at Lambeth Palace, July 6 to August 5, 1908* (London 1908), 176.

42. *Catholic Mind* LXIX: 1252 (April 1971), 39-40, 43.

43. Carolyn M. Craft, "Implications of Infallibility," *Anglican Theological Review* LVI:4 (October 1974), 401-18.

44. See my summary in Ryan and Wright, *op. cit.*, 151-59. Cf. *Mysterium Ecclesiae*, sec. 4: "From what has been said about the extent of and conditions governing the infallibility of the whole people of God and of the Church's Magisterium, it follows that the faithful are in no way permitted to see in the Church merely a fundamental *permanence in truth*, which, as some assert, could be reconciled with errors contained here and there in the proposition that the Church's Magisterium teaches to be held irrevocably." Cf. Avery Dulles, in *America*, August 4, 1973, quoted in *Ecumenical Trends* 2:7 (October 1973), 2: "A purely juridical understanding of infallibility, such as the declaration (*Mysterium Ecclesiae*) here seems to favor, is not theologi-

cally viable. I would hold that the entire Church has a kind of *permanence in the truth* of Christ that may appropriately be called 'infallibility' " (italics added).

45. Bishop Langton Fox, Auxiliary of Menevia, Wales, quoted in Clark and Davey, *op. cit.*, 18; cf. Yves Congar, *Ministères et communion ecclésiale* (Paris 1971), 123ff.

46. *L'Osservatore Romano*, English edition, November 7, 1974, p. 9; cf. *New York Times*, October 27 and 28, 1974.

47. *Catholic Mind*, *op. cit.*, 44; *Papal Primacy and the Universal Church*, ed. P. C. Empie and T. A. Murphy (*Lutherans and Catholics in Dialogue*, vol. V; Minneapolis 1974), 12.

48. *Codex Iuris Canonici* (Vatican edition, 1963), pp. 64-66.

49. English translation: Ottawa, Canada, 1974, secs. 24 and 44, pp. 18 and 26.

50. Dogmatic Constitution on the Church, *Lumen Gentium*, n. 25, in *The Documents of Vatican II*, ed. Walter M. Abbott (N.Y. 1966) p. 48.

51. *Concilium*, Vol. 74, *The Plurality of Ministries*, ed. H. Küng and W. Kasper (N.Y. 1971), 96; cf. *The Tablet* (London), 7 March 1970 and 12 December 1970, pp. 220-21 and 1201-02.

52. Herbert J. Ryan, "Ordained Ministry in Anglican-Roman Catholic Dialogue," *Diakonia* 7:2 (1972), 186.

53. Fr. Avery Dulles has, in fact, already proposed that the anathemas be lifted against those outside the Roman Communion who do not believe in these two Marian dogmas. *Origins* 4:27, December 26, 1974, 417-21.

54. Cf. J. M. R. Tillard, "The Deeper Implications of the Anglican-Roman Catholic Dialogue" in *One in Christ* VIII:3 (1972-3), 256-57.

55. *Dogmatic Theology*, vol. II, *Authority* (N.Y. 1908, rp. 1968 and 1974 by American Church Publications, Pelham Manor, N.Y.), 171.

56. *The Lambeth Conference 1930* (London), 29.

57. *Papal Primacy and the Universal Church*, *op. cit.*, 10.

58. *Ibid.*, 12.

59. "*prokathemene tes agapes.*" *The Apostolic Fathers*, trans. K. Lake, I, 224 (Loeb Classical Library, Cambridge, Mass., 1912).

60. Quoted in n. 89, p. 192, of *Catholic Theological Society of America, Proceedings of the Twenty-Ninth Annual Convention*, vol. 29 (Bronx, N.Y. 1972).

61. Full text printed in *Herder Correspondence* V:12 (December 1968), 372-76.

62. *Documentation Catholique*, vol. 64, no. 1494, May 21, 1967, col. 870; cf. *Osservatore Romano*, 30 April 1967.

63. Each side should realize, of course, that there are some of its members who do in fact believe what is officially the "position" of the other side: thus, there are many Anglicans who in fact believe the Roman dogmas about the immaculate conception and assumption of Mary, even a few who believe in the Pope's infallibility, and certainly many Roman Catholics who are convinced of the validity of Anglican orders!

64. *Op. cit.*, n. 46. Obtainable from Augsburg Publishing House, 426 S. Fifth Street, Minneapolis, Minn. 55415.

65. Avery Dulles, "The Papacy: Bond or Barrier?" in *Origins* 3:45, 710.

66. *The Gospel and the Catholic Church*, *op. cit.*, 64-65.

NOTES ON THE CONTRIBUTORS

Joseph A. Burgess is an assistant professor at the Lutheran Theological Seminary in Gettysburg, Pa. A biblical scholar, he received his doctorate in theology from the University of Basel. He was a contributor to the ecumenical study entitled *Peter in the New Testament* (Augsburg/Paulist).

Avery Dulles, S.J. is professor of systematic theology at The Catholic University of America, Washington, D.C. He is the author of a dozen books in the areas of revelation and ecclesiology. He is a graduate of Harvard and the Gregorian University, Rome.

C. Brownlow Hastings is assistant director of the Department of Interfaith Witness for the Southern Baptist Home Mission Board, Atlanta, Ga. He is a graduate of Baylor and of the Southern Baptist Theological Seminary, Louisville, Ky. He has written a number of articles and books on Scripture and ecumenical subjects.

Ross Mackenzie is John Q. Dickinson Professor of Church History at Union Theological Seminary in Richmond, Virginia. He has been a representative for the Presbyterian Church in the Consultation on Church Union and is the author of a number of textbooks in theology.

John Meyendorff, an Orthodox priest, is professor of church history and patristics at St. Vladimir's Orthodox Theological Seminary, Crestwood, N.Y. and is editor of *St. Vladimir's Theological Quarterly*. He is chairman of the Faith and Order Commission of the World Council of Churches.

J. Robert Nelson is professor of systematic theology at the Boston University School of Theology. He has written widely in the area of Christian ecumenism and since 1967 has been chairman of the Working Committee on Faith and Order of the World Council of Churches. In 1968 he became the first non-Catholic to teach at the Gregorian University in Rome.

J. Robert Wright is professor of church history at the General Theological Seminary in New York. He holds degrees from Emory University in Atlanta, General Theological Seminary, and Oxford.

Ordained in 1964, he has written widely on ecumenical issues and is a member of many church and ecumenical commissions.

Peter J. McCord is a financial consultant and president of First Piedmont Capital Corporation in Greenville, S.C. He attended Holy Cross and has degrees from Fordham, New York University, and the Gregorian University. He has worked as a translator of theological books.

Robert McAfee Brown, a Presbyterian, teaches at Stanford University and is the author of several books on theology and ecumenism, including *The Spirit of Protestantism* and *The Pseudonyms of God*.